Contents

Introduction

Michael Carley

Despite many decades of urban policy and renewal initiatives, the need for social inclusion and urban regeneration in Britain's cities and towns remains pressing. Tackling these fundamental issues is a national, as well as local, challenge. The government, through many initiatives, including the New Commitment to Regeneration, the National Strategy for Neighbourhood Renewal (SEU, 1998), the Urban Task Force (DETR, 1999) and the urban White Paper (DETR, 2000), has indicated its strong commitment to regeneration. Citizens, politicians and professionals are equally committed, working at various spatial levels from the bottom up to the top down.

The Joseph Rowntree Foundation has contributed to this national endeavour through the organisation, funding and management of its Area Regeneration Programme (ARP). This has resulted in 64 practical research projects, based on extensive fieldwork in Britain's cities and towns. The research has covered every aspect of regeneration policy and practice from national to neighbourhood level, and from community development to national labour market analysis.

This report summarises the outcomes of these research projects in terms of the main themes, observations, conclusions and recommendations from the five-year long research programme.

A continuing challenge: achieving prosperity *and* social inclusion

Despite the many decades of regeneration activity since the designation of Housing Action Areas in 1969, the task remains substantial. For example, recent research for the Foundation reveals that

Britain's 20 major cities have lost half a million, mainly male, manufacturing jobs since 1981 (Turok and Edge, 1999). Unfortunately, a striking conclusion from the research is that both relative and absolute declines in employment opportunity have not diminished in the past two decades – despite expectations to the contrary – and there has been a substantial fall in unemployment.

The households in the inner areas of large conurbations have been the worst hit, with steep declines in employment and a large-scale loss of full-time, male manual jobs. But unemployment rates tell only half the story – non-employment in inner-city and industrial areas relative to the rest of the country is greater than suggested by unemployment figures alone (Green and Owen, 1998). There is also a racial dimension, given that more than half of African-Caribbean and Africans and over a third of South Asians live in mixed tenure, inner-city districts with the highest rates of unemployment (Chahal, 2000). The result of this long-discussed process of deindustrialisation is low household income in regeneration areas. Many of these households are experiencing their third generation of male unemployment, with increasingly low aspirations for each succeeding generation. This is a significant factor in social exclusion.

The process of deindustrialisation has been augmented by three related processes, all of which make inner-city regeneration more difficult:

- a **decentralisation of economic activity** as retailing, offices and new single-floor factories moved to suburban and greenfield locations;
- a pronounced **shift of population** from urban areas to suburban locations, market towns and rural areas;

Area Abandonment.

- a **concentration of socially deprived households** in the worst estates and urban neighbourhoods, as prosperous households moved on. One consequence for inner cities has been what is termed 'area abandonment' (Power and Mumford, 1999).

Loss of economic function and the economically-able, mobile segments of the population from the former industrial cities has major impacts on service provision such as education and health, for the residents who remain. As the client base declines while the fixed costs of service delivery remain constant, social problems become concentrated. In cities such as Glasgow or Manchester, where 60% of residents may live in designated regeneration areas, regeneration is not just an area-based task, but city-wide and regional. This makes urban regeneration a national challenge.

Other challenges to regeneration include:

- The need to achieve **sustainability**, or an enduring stream of benefits in regeneration, while in practice, most regeneration initiatives have not achieved lasting benefits and have left people cynical about long-term prospects.
- The need to derive **economic and social renewal**, and social inclusion, from the necessary but more simple task of physical regeneration. A challenge is for physical regeneration to also tackle the impact of manufacturing decline and the loss of manual jobs in industrial cities and towns.
- The **national policy framework** requires continuing innovation towards a more strategic approach which:
  - grapples with urban renewal as a national objective;
  - integrates policy streams and encourages flexible use of mainstream budgets;
  - allocates resources to the investment in infrastructure from schools to public transport; and most importantly
  - devolves real control from the centre to the regional, city and local levels.
- The need to link national policy, regional and sub-regional governance, city-level strategy and local action in a **coherent spatial development framework** so that top-down and bottom-up initiatives are mutually supportive.

- The need to **harness mainstream policy and services** to regeneration requirements, given that more than 90% of public expenditure in regeneration areas is through mainstream budgets. Mainstream programmes need to achieve better integration with the temporary, 'catalyst' funding streams which characterise regeneration programmes. In turn, regeneration funding regimes need to be joined-up – probably at the regional level.
- The need to promote a potentially fruitful convergence of interests between regeneration and the government's agenda for the **modernisation of local government**. An important task of the modernisation agenda is to develop local democracy and neighbourhood initiatives to balance what is mainly a top-down approach to area regeneration often accompanied by only problematic or tokenistic participation exercises.
- The need to **broaden the base of partnerships** to include necessary partners such as the Benefits Agency, health authorities, the police and the Employment Service.
- The need to **empower local neighbourhoods** to play a valid, continuing role in neighbourhood management. Local government modernisation is essential for allowing neighbourhoods to oversee services, while redefining the role of the local authority in a wholly constructive manner.

Looking for signposts: what to do and how to do it

Recently, there has been much useful analysis of urban problems, including that by the Urban Task Force (DETR, 1999), the Social Exclusion Unit (SEU, 1998), the Scottish Social Exclusion Network, leading up to a new Urban White Paper for England and Wales. But this analysis has focused more on what we ought to do, and rather less on the equally important question of how we are going to do it. This distinction mirrors the important relationship between regeneration strategy and partnership: *the what to do and the how to do it*. Certainly, strategy derived in the absence of a partnership, however logical and intelligent, is likely to be largely ignored by key stakeholders because they have not had a hand in fashioning it and thus have no sense of ownership. But 'talking shop' partnerships, which are not grappling with real strategic issues, waste

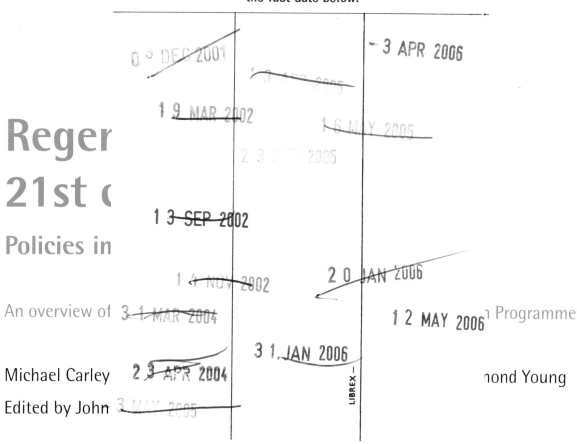

Reger
21st c

Policies in

An overview of ... Programme

Michael Carley ... nond Young

Edited by John

The POLICY
PP
PRESS

First published in Great Britain in December 2000 by

The Policy Press
34 Tyndall's Park Road
Bristol BS8 1PY
UK

Tel no +44 (0)117 954 6800
Fax no +44 (0)117 973 7308
E-mail tpp@bristol.ac.uk
www.policypress.org.uk

© The Policy Press and the Joseph Rowntree Foundation 2000

Published for the Joseph Rowntree Foundation by The Policy Press

ISBN 1 86134 308 6

Michael Carley is Professor in the School of Planning and Housing, Heriot-Watt University, **Mike Campbell** is Director of the Policy Research Unit, Leeds Metropolitan University, **Ade Kearns** is Head of Department, and **Raymond Young** is Honorary Senior Research Fellow, both at the Department of Urban Studies, University of Glasgow, **Martin Wood** is a freelance researcher, and **John Low** is Research Manager for the Area Regeneration Programme, Joseph Rowntree Foundation.

The **Joseph Rowntree Foundation** has supported this project as part of its programme of research and innovative development projects, which it hopes will be of value to policy makers, practitioners and service users. The facts presented and views expressed in this report are, however, those of the authors and not necessarily those of the Foundation.

Cover design by Qube Design Associates, Bristol
Front cover photographs kindly supplied by www.johnbirdsall.co.uk and Karen Bowler, The Policy Press
Printed in Great Britain by Hobbs the Printers Ltd, Southampton

partners' valuable time, financial resources and bring the partnership approach into disrepute. The quality of regeneration strategy and the quality of partnership are intimately related.

Area Regeneration Programme: learning-by-doing is the key

The ARP has steadfastly considered both the what to do and the how to do it better, in combination. It does not, however, suggest that there are easy or quick answers. Rather there are signposts and frameworks that can help people work towards solutions. Learning-by-doing is the key – mechanisms for moving forward do not have to be perfect on day one; the complexity of the problems faced ensures that this is unlikely. However, we must be committed, as a nation, to learning from experience, in both formal and informal ways. Inspired leadership is necessary and obstacles at all levels must be honestly identified and overcome. Starting from the perspective of the community or the neighbourhood, working out effective routes to make the vital linkage connecting bottom up with top down is an exciting challenge to both regeneration and to revitalising local democracy in Britain.

Based almost entirely on fieldwork looking at cities and the activities of partners in regeneration, the ARP represents part of this important process of learning-by-doing. This summary report documents that learning, setting out the key points from the many research projects. It also points the interested reader to more detailed information in the many published research reports, their summaries, called 'Findings', and periodic broader reviews of related research projects, in the Foundations series. Information on these is given in the Appendix.

Organisation of this report

This report is set out as follows. Each chapter summarises a key theme in the research programme, beginning with a box which summarises the key observations to arise from the research projects and the policy implications thereof. These themes are listed overleaf with the page numbers for the appropriate summary box.

What's the problem? Patterns, processes and perceptions

Ade Kearns

Summary

In this chapter, we look at the nature of the problems which area regeneration has to tackle. Recent trends and geographical patterns are described in relation to employment and unemployment, area deprivation, neighbourhood dissatisfaction, low housing demand, and public and private sector service withdrawal. Some of the underlying processes causing these patterns are examined. The role of people's perceptions is considered in two ways. First, residents' views of regeneration initiatives are reported: do residents' feel involved and do they get what they want out of regeneration? Second, the importance of people's perceptions of regeneration areas is shown through a study of estate images.

Policy implications

The findings have many implications for policy makers and practitioners, but the most important are:

- There are indications that urban policy can influence the location of employment through investment in the urban fabric and infrastructure, and the re-use of derelict land for prepared industrial sites, but systematic information on comparative city performance is required to provide a better evidence base for this approach

- New approaches to neighbourhood renewal and management should be considered in relation to most neighbourhoods if quality of life and the sustainability of urban areas is to be enhanced

- Policies to tackle low demand and area abandonment in the future will have to pay much more attention to problems in the private sector and issues of mainstream services

- The government should specify *minimum standards for neighbourhood services and amenities* across Britain, perhaps adjusted according to neighbourhood population; national policy targets for local neighbourhoods would then be clear

- Community control and influence in regeneration needs to be enhanced; means of acknowledging, rewarding and paying for resident involvement should also be considered

- Regeneration initiatives need to engage in media and image management, persuading influential actors that they have a stake in the enhancement of an area's reputation

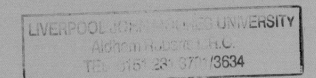

Patterns and processes of decline and disadvantage

The Area Regeneration Programme (ARP) studied patterns and processes of decline and disadvantage in relation to three phenomena, namely, employment and unemployment, area deprivation, and low demand and abandonment in marginal areas.

Employment and unemployment

Issues of the geography of employment were considered by two ARP studies. While Turok and Edge (1999) considered changes in the numbers of jobs located in Britain's cities, Green and Owen (1998) analysed rates of non-employment by local authority district (LAD) and travel-to-work-area (TTWA).

Non-employment: a regional divide

In order to understand *who* is not working *where*, Green and Owen (1998) argue for a wider focus beyond unemployment to non-employment. The non-employed include, not only the registered unemployed, but also those who are economically inactive and want a job, whether or not they are seeking work.

Green and Owen found significant evidence of strong regional differences in the dynamics of non-employment over the 1981-96 period, as follows:

- The regions of East Anglia, the South West, East Midlands and the South East (excluding London) experienced below average rates of male non-employment, while the North, the North West, Wales, Scotland, Yorkshire and Humberside and the West Midlands experienced above average rates, sometimes 15-20% above the national average.
- While regional rates of unemployment have converged over time, regional rates of inactivity have not.
- Local authorities classified as 'mining and industrial areas' (such as in Clydeside, Wales, Durham and Yorkshire) had the highest rates of non-employment in both 1981 and 1991, with increase over time due solely to a growth in inactivity among men of working age.
- TTWAs from southern Britain experienced disproportionately favourable circumstances with a high likelihood of people ceasing to be unemployed, and many also having a low likelihood of becoming unemployed in the first place. TTWAs in northern Britain, and covering the largest cities, dominated the unfavourable areas with a high risk of becoming unemployed and a low risk of ceasing to be unemployed.
- Comparing like with like, northern areas (urban and rural) experience higher incidences of longer-term unemployment (six months or more) than southern areas at *most levels of the urban hierarchy*, and the highest incidences are in large northern and sub-dominant cities. Thus, the regional divide is not entirely explained by the presence of large cities in the north.

Manufacturing employment decline in cities

Turok and Edge (1999) used the government's Annual Employment Survey from 1981 to 1996 to study employment change by industry for Britain's cities compared with other areas.

The results show a continuing urban–rural shift in employment around our cities, with the loss of jobs in urban cores being mainly due to a persistent decline in manufacturing activity. The larger cities were poor performers and lost 5% of their jobs (500,000). There has also been a relative decentralisation of jobs within urban areas. The core districts of the conurbations lost 12% of their jobs over the period, while the outer districts lost only 2%.

Employment in manufacturing has declined everywhere, but up to twice as fast in the conurbations than in the smaller cities, towns and rural areas. Furthermore, the rate of growth in private service employment was much slower in the conurbations (at 20%), than in the towns and rural areas (at nearly 50%). Growth in emerging sectors which make up the knowledge economy, cultural industries and consumer services had not yet shown signs of being sufficient to compensate for the loss of manufacturing and manual employment in cities.

The influence of structural and local factors on employment

The change in employment in different towns and cities can be broken down into three elements:

national, structural (industrial mix) and local factors. Such an analysis for the period 1981-91 shows:

- Most conurbation cores had favourable industrial structures, but this positive effect was outweighed by the negative effect of their local attributes – possibly physical constraints; the poor performance of the urban cores is not explained by a 'decline in traditional industries'.
- Some free-standing cities (such as Stoke, Coventry and Doncaster) do, however, perform poorly due to an unfavourable industrial structure.
- Other free-standing cities (such as Cardiff, Bristol and Edinburgh) enjoy very favourable industrial mixes.
- Property and infrastructure may be important to a city's performance: a lack of suitable sites for business expansion may be hindering the conurbation cores, while investment in the physical fabric and redevelopment of derelict land could explain the positive local effect on employment change in Leeds – unique among the conurbation cores.

Urban labour market adjustments

Constructing labour market accounts for cities, Turok and Edge identify the most significant response to urban job losses as being an increase in net out-migration, which reduced the cities male labour supply by 7% and female supply by 4% during the 1980s. This is a selective process, removing white-collar and younger employed people rather than assisting manual workers and the non-employed. Those urban residents most vulnerable to job losses do not, in general, out-migrate from cities.

The second largest response within the labour market has been an expansion of the economically inactive, which reduced the cities labour supply by 5% from 1981-91. The growth in inactivity is greatest among the least skilled and the over 50s and includes a substantial group of the 'hidden unemployed' who might really be available for, or seeking, work. The increase in inactivity was greatest in those cities where job loss was highest, suggesting that demand-side factors influence inactivity and permanent sickness.

Overall, out-commuting from cities makes a small contribution to reducing urban unemployment – around 25%. 'Reverse commuting' by city residents is low and commuting distances for most people in cities are short. Thus, employment growth in satellite centres and semi-rural and rural areas is unlikely to help inner-urban residents, even if urban transportation was improved.

Policy implications

The ARP studies of spatial patterns of non-employment and employment change in cities have the following policy implications:

- Urban and regional policy needs to explicitly acknowledge that there has been a city employment problem and a regional divide in the experience of employment change and non-employment. There are already concerns that in its response to the Education and Employment Select Committee's report on *Employability and jobs* (Education and Employment Committee, 2000), the government has not adequately addressed the issue of lack of demand for employment.
- Closer attention needs to be paid to tracking the jobs gap in cities and regions. We do not know whether the jobs gap is maintained or narrowed during periods of national employment growth such as the late 1990s. Independent monitoring is required.
- Employment, business and unemployment policies should have a stronger focus on prevention rather than cure (that is, reducing the risk of becoming unemployed in the first place rather than trying to increase the rate of re-employment), and on supporting business expansion as well as start-ups.
- An over-emphasis on the industries of the 'new economy' should not be at the expense of acknowledging the need for an expansion of manual and manufacturing employment in many urban areas.
- An urban policy which focuses on urban design, quality of life and environmental issues is unlikely to stem the flow of out-migration from city cores, since the evidence suggests that such out-migration follows or parallels the urban–rural shift in employment. Thus, inner-urban job expansion is crucial.
- There are indications that urban policy can influence the location of employment through investment in the urban fabric and infrastructure, and the re-use of derelict land for prepared industrial sites. However, further

3

monitoring and evaluation of the relationship between such investment and policies on the one hand and differential urban economic performance on the other is required to provide a better evidence-base for this approach.

- The local, spatial operation of urban labour markets in Britain needs closer scrutiny. Urban and regional policy makers must be aware of the reality of patterns of inter- and intra-urban commuting and of issues of geographical access to employment opportunities for different skill groups so that economic development and transport policies are more attuned to actual labour market behaviour. Only in this way can we establish what might constitute a beneficial spatial pattern of employment growth, for example, in relation to the long-term unemployed.

Area deprivation and disadvantage

Neighbourhood dissatisfaction and area disadvantage

Burrows and Rhodes (1998) used the Survey of English Housing (SEH) to identify dissatisfaction within neighbourhoods. They found that over a fifth of respondents consider crime and vandalism to be a major problem in their area – by far the most prevalent concern. After this, came inadequate leisure facilities (rated a major issue by 15% of respondents) and issues of environmental nuisance, such as problems with dogs and litter. Some of the issues which appear more frequently in the media are less prevalent as major local problems, for example, schools, problem neighbours and noise.

As well as identifying major local issues, the study highlighted which groups are most likely to be dissatisfied with their neighbourhood. A combined analysis showed high rates of neighbourhood dissatisfaction among: the unemployed and economically inactive in social housing (27% dissatisfied), especially if they were living in the North East (42%) or London, Yorkshire and the North West (30%); and among the semi-skilled living in private renting in London, Yorkshire, the North East and the North West (35% dissatisfied). A major conclusion of the study is that problematic neighbourhoods are not the preserve of the social rented sector, but are

also experienced by homeowners and private renters. Thus:

> ... any area regeneration targeting of the 'worst estates' will miss a significant proportion of households living in what they themselves perceive to be squalid neighbourhoods [sic]. (Burrows and Rhodes, 1998, p 32)

These sociodemographic indicators of area dissatisfaction were used to estimate the incidence of neighbourhood dissatisfaction in local areas around Britain. According to the 'geography of misery', many of the districts and wards with the highest rates of area dissatisfaction lie in London and the North East and are either coalfield areas or port and heavy industry districts with concentrations of social housing. This distribution of neighbourhood dissatisfaction does not coincide with the Index of Local Conditions used by the Department of the Environment, Transport and the Regions (DETR) for resource allocation and policy prioritisation.

Finally, the authors urge policy makers and researchers to relate neighbourhood influences to a range of social outcomes, which is an important yet underdeveloped field of urban analysis in the UK.

Deprived areas and housing tenure

Lee and Murie (1997) argue that an index is to be preferred to single indicators of deprivation for targeting of poor areas. They also demonstrate that the identification of disadvantaged local areas varies markedly according to which index is used.

Based on earlier work to identify the most robust index of deprivation (Lee et al, 1995), Lee and Murie analysed the Breadline Britain index for districts across Britain and at ward level within five cities. Their findings were that:

- The most deprived districts lie in London, Clydeside, Tyne and Wear and the North West – as before, the pattern is dominated by London and the northern conurbations.
- Deprived districts include declining industrial areas, declining coastal towns, seaside towns and rural areas with fragile economies.
- Within cities, inequality between neighbourhoods increased between 1981 and 1991.

MACDONALD & HAYS.

- The relationship between deprivation and housing tenure varies between cities. In some cities (such as Edinburgh and Liverpool) there is a close match, but in others there is not (such as Bradford and Birmingham). In some cities, council estates have lower levels of deprivation than areas of older owner-occupation and private renting. In other districts (for example, Tower Hamlets) the more important issue is which council housing estates to target.
- Spatial patterns of deprivation between the inner and outer city also vary. For example, in Edinburgh, deprivation is highest in peripheral council housing estates, but there is also a concentration of deprivation in the city centre. In Birmingham, on the other hand, deprivation is greatest in a ring around the city centre and in the inner suburbs, rather than in peripheral council housing areas.

Policy implications

The findings from the ARP research into patterns of area deprivation and disadvantage have the following implications for neighbourhood renewal policies:

- Policy must be clear on its priorities for tackling joblessness, poverty, deprivation and neighbourhood disadvantage, since the distribution of resources to tackle these issues will differ both nationally and locally. Furthermore, the role of national measures of deprivation in targeting resources to districts and regions needs to be carefully specified and justified. There must be scope for the local identification of priority deprived neighbourhoods for area interventions.
- The forthcoming DETR Index of Deprivation does not appear to adequately cover the range of neighbourhood quality issues addressed in the 'geography of misery' (Burrows and Rhodes, 1998), dealing only with access to service items. This raises the question of whether neighbourhood dissatisfaction is considered to be a form of deprivation.
- The smaller the scale at which we can identify and appreciate (dis)advantaged areas the better. Our understanding and definition of neighbourhoods needs to be improved. Consideration should be given to the possibility of a bottom-up approach to the definition of locally acknowledged neighbourhood areas for policy intervention

and monitoring purposes. For example, in Greater Easterhouse in Glasgow, regeneration managers drew up neighbourhood boundaries based on knowledge and experience, but then adjusted them in light of residents' comments.
- A long-term research strategy should be developed to identify, evaluate and monitor the potential mechanisms through which neighbourhood conditions might affect social outcomes and health and well-being for individuals, households and groups.
- An approach which combines target areas with 'floor targets' applicable to mainstream services and agencies for all areas should be adopted. This would allow combined and integrated action in the very worst areas while also seeking to safeguard other vulnerable areas from decline in particular services or conditions.
- Considerable resources are required to tackle even a modest definition of the most deprived neighbourhoods in Britain over a reasonable period of time.
- Neither area deprivation nor neighbourhood dissatisfaction are the sole preserve of council housing estates, but are also significant features of other housing tenures and different types of neighbourhood. New approaches to neighbourhood renewal and management should be considered in relation to most neighbourhoods if quality of life and the sustainability of urban areas is to be enhanced.

Low demand for housing and area abandonment

The national picture

Power and Mumford (1999) report that "there is evidence of falling and changing demand for social housing in many areas of the country – in regions of housing shortage as well as surplus" (p ix). While this may be true, Holmans and Simpson (1999) showed that, in the 1990s, the levels of vacancies and departures from local authority housing – key indicators of low demand – rose more in the North of England, and to a lesser extent the Midlands, than in the South. In all regions the highest vacancy and departure rates are in metropolitan districts and former industrial cities. There is much higher demand in small towns, suburbs and more rural areas.

Analysis of population change shows that there has been an increase in net outward migration from the North of England, West Midlands and Scotland to the South of England – probably related to job opportunities – but that the number of households in the North of England is still projected to increase. Thus, low demand is not a symptom of a shortfall of household formation and its incidence will be localised.

The availability of houses to buy at low prices partly explains the incidence of low demand for social housing. The evidence also shows greater household movement with more people taking up social housing tenancies. However, people reside in the social rented sector for shorter periods of time and there are more transfers between properties within the sector. Social renting is increasingly seen as a temporary status rather than a housing career.

Local problems

Power and Mumford (1999) looked in depth at the incidence of low demand for housing and incipient area abandonment in four inner neighbourhoods in Manchester and Newcastle. These were areas experiencing rapid decline, with population losses 2-3 times the city average rate in the case of Manchester, and 5-10 times the city rate in the case of the two Newcastle neighbourhoods. The main manifestations of the problem were:

- an increase in the number of empty, unwanted properties;
- a scattering of demolition sites throughout the neighbourhoods;
- plummeting property values and low Right-to-Buy sales;
- very high residency turnover rates of between 20% and 50% per annum in particular blocks or estates;
- poor environments and no overall plan, constituting a sense of dereliction and of being uncared for;
- disruption and disorder.

The roots of abandonment

The context in which urban abandonment occurs includes:

- an historic poor reputation for an area;
- relative industrial decline and job losses;

- an oversupply of council housing estates;
- poor management of estates;
- easy access to affordable owner-occupation in suburban greenfield developments.

A different perspective was presented by Richardson and Corbishley's (1999) study of frequent moving in the West End of Newcastle. This is a slum clearance, 'twilight zone' area in which social problems became more prominent in the 1980s, and where the housing market finally collapsed in the 1990s. Housing tenure in the area is split 63/27% social and private housing with a 25% void rate. Frequent movers reside in the locality in these circumstances.

Most frequent movers moved for personal reasons to do with trying – and often failing – to form stable relationships, and for reasons related to neighbour harassment and poor housing conditions. Frequent movers had traumatic childhoods, left home at an early age, had children at a young age, and often experienced violence from their partners. The local housing surplus enabled their frequent moving, but the prevention of movement may not be a good thing, given the personal circumstances of many of the households involved.

Policy implications

Power and Mumford locate the dominance of social housing within these neighbourhoods at the heart of the problem. Council housing today repels young people wishing to enter homeownership and deters investment in owner-occupation within the neighbourhoods. Further, the council sector has concentrated socially excluded people, thus exacerbating problems. There has been a continuing trend towards a lower-income social rented sector in the 1990s, with council housing becoming a sector for older people, the unemployed, female-headed households and those with no choice in housing (Lee and Murie, 1997).

Power and Mumford offer a four-fold prescription for reversing the urban decline represented by low demand and area abandonment, including reorienting social housing. The overall aim is to attract back into cities more people in work with higher incomes and higher skills, and to prevent further exodus by stabilising community conditions in inner areas.

Four-fold strategy to tackle low demand

- Pro-urban policies and investment by the government is needed, in particular in relation to the environment and economic development. Holmans and Simpson (1999) also argue that regional policy may be forced back onto the agenda on the grounds that:

  > accommodating extra people, including regional migrants, in the southern half of the country will be difficult;
  > there is unused infrastructure in the north of the country;
  > poor economic prospects for people in less favoured regions is inequitable.

- The development of mixed urban communities and the attraction of 'urban pioneers' through higher densities and mixed-used neighbourhoods, to live alongside stable residents supported to remain.

- Improved neighbourhood management and leadership, together with the localisation of mainstream services, especially pro-active street policing.

- The better marketing of social housing in tandem with its reorientation through new, non-profit landlords.

Power and Mumford argue that social housing needs to be marketed to a wide band of people in order to raise its value and increase demand; it should be opened up to less precarious tenants. This is a major challenge to the conventional role of social housing founded on needs-based allocation. They argue for broad eligibility criteria in social housing allocations, such as people below a certain income level, with the aim of achieving a greater social mix. We can note that Holmans and Simpson (1999) contend that the degree of choice available in social housing allocations can exacerbate problems of unpopularity and be destabilising. Lastly, social housing should also be made less visible through high quality, integrative design policies.

The frequent movers research, however, indicates that instability within inner-city areas might have social roots for which housing interventions are not the primary solution. Early interventions of a preventative nature are needed, as well as management solutions to facilitate moves and help communities cope with residential change.

In reviewing these prescriptions, it is clear that there are competing agendas and challenges for policy:

- The stress on social housing, and, in particular, council housing estates, runs the risk of diverting attention from the fact that some low-demand areas may consist of up to 50% private sector housing, and local concentrations of deprivation occur in all housing tenures. Social housing policies will not tackle these problems. For Lee and Murie, future policies "will have to pay much more attention to problems in the private sector" (1997, p 54).

- The research and policy is focused on the difficulties of 'estates'. One must be doubtful about the success of any wider marketing of estates. Despite much of what is proposed, council estates would be in danger of remaining just that – estates – unless radical restructuring is undertaken alongside rebranding initiatives (see Dean and Hastings, 2000).

- The identification of 'urban pioneers' needs to be specific in terms of who they are, how their needs can be met, and what their impacts will be. More attention needs to be given to retaining out-migrating middle-income families.

- Power and Mumford (1999) stress the need to save and not jeopardise inner areas, while both they and Holmans and Simpson (1999) question the 'worst first' approach to regeneration, preferring to "hold conditions in precarious areas" (Power and Mumford, 1999, p 92) and engage in "preventative measures ... at arresting decline in areas where demand is still reasonably healthy" (Holmans and Simpson, 1999, p 79). This leaves unresolved the issue of how urban regeneration policy might decide whether, and in what circumstances, permitted or managed decline of an area is the right approach, and how implementation could be handled sensitively. Can policy save everywhere? Should policy assume that abandonment and demolition will be 'inevitable' in some areas?

- There is a tension between the push for national analysis and policies and the reality of responding to local circumstances. Lee and Murie argue for local analysis and initiatives linked to city-wide strategies, rather than simple national policy responses. The frequent mover researchers also support localised solutions at the neighbourhood level. Clearly, we need to better understand the causes of neighbourhood decline – *which will vary* – to know whether the solution(s) lie in housing and the environment; education and other mainstream services; or employment, for example. As Niner (1999) says in her summary of research into low demand housing:

> ... managing or avoiding low demand for housing is a prime candidate for 'joined-up thinking'.... There are no easy, ready-made answers for all circumstances. What 'works' in some places does not necessarily work everywhere and for everyone....
> (p 6)

Service withdrawal and exclusion

Another form of abandonment is the withdrawal of services from poor people and poor areas. In *Service not included*, Speak and Graham (2000) illustrated the extent of exclusion in relation to energy, telecommunications, retail banking and shopping which occurred in two neighbourhoods in Liverpool and Manchester. Financial and social impacts of service exclusion were identified.

The impacts of service exclusion

There are four types of impact of service withdrawal:

- The **financial costs** of service exclusion included having to borrow money at higher interest rates from licensed money-lenders or through mail order shopping; paying higher tariffs for energy via pre-payment meters; and paying higher prices for lower quality food items at local shops.
- The **transactional costs** of service exclusion include the extra effort the excluded have to put in to basic tasks. Rather than living 'friction free' everyday lives, the excluded have to cover the distance between themselves and providers to access services or sort out problems.
- The **social costs** of service exclusion included alienation from up-market city centre shopping districts and difficulties in obtaining and retaining a job without a telephone, bank account or home contents insurance.

- Where more than one type of service access problem existed, **compound exclusion** could result through knock-on effects, with a serious impact on residents' quality of life.

Additional effects of service withdrawal on the local landscape and its psychological impacts on individuals and communities were highlighted by Wood and Vamplew (1999) who studied the St Hilda's area in Middlesbrough, and by Andersen et al (1999) who studied the Speke Estate in Liverpool. The trend of closures and neglect had several psychological impacts on the communities, affecting their morale and outlook.

Psychological effects of neighbourhood decline

- A **loss of pride** as some of the lost functions and buildings had given the area poor status.
- A **loss of identity** as landmark buildings which constituted the area's architectural and industrial heritage were being destroyed or allowed to deteriorate. Guilt accompanied the awareness that this heritage would not be passed on to future generations.
- A **loss of self-sufficiency**. Where once the neighbourhood supported most functions, now people had to travel off the estate for a range of daily functions.
- **Pessimism** and a belief that the authorities had no stake in the area's future and would allow it to 'die'.
- A **sense of betrayal** that the owners and authorities had "just left it to fall to bits".

Policy implications

Speak and Graham (2000) illustrate how the policy arena at both national and local levels can respond to problems of service withdrawal and exclusion in regeneration areas. A four-fold approach is recommended:

> ***Regulation:*** Private service industries need to be forced through regulation to reduce the impacts of their spatial and operational restructuring on marginalised groups.

> ***Community provision:*** National policy needs to support alternative community enterprises by secure funding, adequate training and encouragement to private firms to work with community initiatives by providing advice and expertise and offering partnership contracts for work.

Reversing 'over-abandonment': Specialised service packages for people in disadvantaged areas could be developed with national policy support and through partnerships among providers of different services (such as transport and retailing, or retailing and banks). In this way, new markets can be developed and the costs of outlets or 'service platforms' reduced. Public bodies and local authorities could also use their bargaining power in contract situations to obtain commitments from providers to offer services in poor areas. *Recalculating welfare benefits:* Benefits should be more locally sensitive, with higher levels of award to people living in higher cost areas: actual costs under marginalised conditions need to be taken into account.

Speak and Graham argue for better measurement of private service use across the country. To this we might add that the government should specify *minimum standards for neighbourhood services and amenities* across Britain, perhaps adjusted according to neighbourhood population. National policy targets for local neighbourhoods would then be clear, for example, that every defined neighbourhood should have a safe play area, or that every community above a certain size should have a supermarket within 15-minutes travelling time. In order to help meet these threshold standards for neighbourhood services, a fund should exist to subsidise service outlets; the notion of revenue subsidies for Post Offices or rural petrol stations could be extended to other aspects of the minimum neighbourhood service provision guidelines.

The historic identity of neighbourhoods and communities should be preserved with a requirement placed on local authorities to maintain and find alternative uses for important local buildings protected under *community preservation orders*.

Perceptions in and of regeneration areas

The ARP included two types of study of perceptions pertaining to regeneration areas, namely, an investigation of residents' views of regeneration programmes, and, second, a study of the significance and impacts of negative images of disadvantaged areas and of ways to tackle an area's poor reputation.

Perceptions of regeneration

Four projects, studying eight neighbourhoods, reported on residents' views of the regeneration process. Similar issues arose in East London (Cattell and Evans, 1999), Liverpool (Andersen et al, 1999), Teesside (Wood and Vamplew, 1999) and Nottingham (Silburn et al, 1999). Alongside positive views of change, there was also scepticism about the effectiveness of regeneration programmes.

Resentment existed of the involvement of regeneration professionals in people's lives and communities. There was a suspicion that professionals were the ones to gain from regeneration programmes and concern that local people were used as an unpaid resource; they had skills and knowledge to offer which should be paid for. New partnerships in regeneration areas were sometimes resented by local organisations whose role they were seen to be usurping.

The effectiveness of consultation and involvement

The view which emerged from the studies was that:

- in some areas, residents' awareness of regeneration activities was low;
- communication with non-active residents was poor, either by their representatives or by the professionals;
- there was suspicion that devolved power was a myth: too often, residents did not feel in control of events, and felt even less in control of expenditure decisions;
- consultation arrangements were often inadequate: residents' felt that their questions were not answered, their issues not followed up, decisions were made in other forums, and their own priorities for everyday issues of service provision and social facilities were ignored in favour of large development activities;
- residents felt that they had not had their say despite traditional representative arrangements.

Policy implications

Improvements in the practice of regeneration are needed in several areas.

- Regeneration must recognise that neighbourhoods contain diverse groups and sometimes more than one community. This will affect the type, location and operation of facilities and amenities within the area and is important to achieving social cohesion rather than perpetuating divisions.
- Government and regeneration partnerships must evaluate how, and to what extent, the community can be given control over regeneration strategies and budgets. Resources to support community-owned structures, agendas and projects are means by which diversity can be accommodated and power shared (Anastacio et al, 2000).
- Means of acknowledging, rewarding and paying for resident involvement should be considered; the high value placed on training by residents is important.
- Structures and processes of consultation and involvement must be geared to greater community influence, be more democratic and accountable and be capable of accommodating multiple community agendas rather than a single professional agenda.
- Improvements in communication with residents is necessary so that people are aware of developments and those developments have a better chance of making the impact that they should.
- Mainstream services must be tied into regeneration agendas more effectively, with commitments to find ways of reversing past closures and withdrawals from disadvantaged areas.

Perceptions of disadvantaged areas and housing estates

The poor image of regeneration areas often persists, despite substantial change. In their study of three estates (in Birmingham, Edinburgh and North Tyneside), Dean and Hastings (2000) show how excluded areas suffer from a deteriorating view of social housing in general, as well as having a specific, poor local reputation. To date, regeneration programmes have not managed, in the main, to shift the images of deprived areas, but management of images is essential if regeneration is to be sustainable.

The impacts of a poor reputation

The following impacts can be identified:

- **Economic impacts** such as higher costs and discrimination when looking for a job.
- **Relationship impacts** such as reduced social contacts, disparaging comments and new relationships put under strain by stereotypes.
- **Service delivery impacts** such as lower-quality services, delivered less frequently and at higher costs, with less choice.
- **Emotional impacts** wherein residents feel angry, hurt and upset by stigma, and may choose to respond by accepting, avoiding, rejecting or challenging the estate's reputation depending on their own attitudes and resources.

There is no single image of an estate, but rather there are varied images among both residents and non-residents. The research identified three groups of residents (committed stayers, potential leavers and probable leavers) and three groups of non-residents (budding incomers, doubtful incomers and improbable incomers).

Dean and Hastings argue that a wide range of actors and agencies contribute to an estate's image by their behaviours, including residents, public and private services, and the media. However, the key services which shape estate images are schools, leisure services, estate agents and the local media. While a large proportion of the negative associations ascribed to the estates relate to the poor environment and amenities, views about the people and criminal behaviour are not far behind (for example, that residents are lazy, have inadequate parents, lack respect for authority). These are the predominant associations among those who reject the estates outright.

Policy implications

Dean and Hastings propose five elements of an approach to improving the negative images of estates:

Appointing an image manager responsible for the image of the estate with authority over public agencies and influence over the private sector. This could be the neighbourhood manager with additional skills in marketing and public relations.

Persuading stakeholders to change their attitude towards the estate either for altruistic or self-interested reasons. Private actors – the potential saboteurs – need to be informed about changes, shown how their own activities can benefit from a positive attitude to the estates, and recruited to act as advocates for the estates.

Managing the media through nurturing relationships with journalists by feeding them exclusive stories with a positive slant, and by communicating clearly in press releases which focus on human interest stories.

Targeting marketing communication to different resident and non-resident groups identified according to their likely response to specific messages. This is both about retaining existing residents and attracting people from neighbouring areas.

Making regeneration more visible by combining early demolition of high-rise or deck-access blocks with redevelopment on visible sights such as traffic corridors and the use of billboards and banners at strategic points.

Drawing non-residents onto estates through a mixture of road and infrastructure changes to reduce physical isolation and the provision of attractive facilities is also recommended. This echoes Forrest and Kearns (1999) suggestion that *excluded estates* need to become *permeable places* and further illustrates the need for regeneration initiatives to be coordinated with city and regional development strategies.

2

Community involvement and capacity building

Martin Wood

Summary
- A long-term commitment involving sustained community development and training is required to enable local people to develop and implement the programmes they need.

- Given the harsh reality of their experience it is a testament to individual strength that so many residents become actively and voluntarily involved in the affairs of their neighbourhood.

- If communities are excluded at the beginning of regeneration programmes then there is a serious danger that the wrong issues will be prioritised.

- Regeneration agencies have failed to ensure the inclusion of all as a result of:
    - an inadequate investment of time and resources;
    - an ignorance of or lack of commitment to equal opportunities;
    - the formality of proceedings and the 'exclusive' nature of the language used.

- Training is required for policy makers and regeneration professionals to facilitate a change in organisational culture and management style.

- The new Neighbourhood Management proposals present exciting opportunities for community involvement in regeneration, but there is a clear tension between having someone in charge and the principle of community involvement.

- The improved management of neighbourhoods will ultimately only succeed if the underlying problems of joblessness and inequality are also tackled.

- Regional or national networks of community organisations will be required to facilitate community involvement at all spatial levels.

Policy implications
- Additional funds should be targeted at community groups and application procedures simplified.

- Levels of community participation should be audited by funders.

- A renewed commitment to community development is required; this should involve an evaluation of competency and an increase in training and management support.

- Residents' service organisations should be explored as a model for Neighbourhood Management to ensure that local people can 'own' or take the lead in renewal efforts.

- Further policies are required to support self-help and mutual aid initiatives such as Local Exchange Trading Schemes (LETS).

- Benefit reforms should redress increasing inequality since local residents can only fully engage in their neighbourhoods when they have more control over their lives.

Why community involvement?

Findings from the Joseph Rowntree Foundation's ARP assert that involving the community produces better results. It is claimed, for example, that local people, drawing on their experiences of life, are best placed to identify the issues that need to be addressed. This means that needs can be targeted accurately and more relevant initiatives developed. It is suggested that, when communities 'own' the solutions, the results are more sustainable than those that have been imposed from outside. Community involvement is not a 'bolt-on' or 'cosmetic' activity (JRF, 1999): successful area regeneration can *only* occur when local people are involved in the process and are equipped with the skills they need in order to have an impact.

Few people, if any, appear to disagree with these sentiments. Unfortunately, however, interpretation and implementation can often leave much to be desired. All too often 'regeneration professionals' wish to decide what role the community should play, who should play it and how they should play it (Anastacio et al, 2000). Most people recognise the apocryphal tale of the tenants who, having been consulted on the colour scheme of their newly refurbished homes, were informed that it had been decided that they would all get the same. Simply consulting residents is a long way removed from genuine community involvement. So what are the barriers that need to be overcome and what are the pitfalls that regeneration projects need to avoid? How should community involvement and capacity building overcome social exclusion? What part should it play in the new 'neighbourhood management' agenda? And what are the geographical levels at which it should operate?

Community involvement can take many forms, from relatively low levels, for example, when local residents are provided with information or consulted through questionnaires or public meetings, to higher levels of engagement, when residents are involved in the decision-making process and actively participate in (or even control) the process of regeneration. The level of community involvement is influenced by a number of factors, including:

- the source of the original impetus for the regeneration initiative;
- the strength and status of existing community groups;
- the level of direct community work support being given to local groups;
- the amenability of the regeneration professionals;
- the organisational culture of the lead agencies or local authority.

When the initiative comes from an external agency or the local authority, particular care needs to be taken to ensure that the views of local people are not discounted or undermined.

Capacity building is increasingly considered to be an important precursor to effective involvement and refers to the process of developing the abilities of local people to organise themselves so that they have more influence over the process and involvement in the outcomes. It stems from a recognition that the pace and nature of regeneration initiatives can contrive to exclude local input. As Duncan and Thomas note, capacity building "helps [local people] better define and achieve their objectives ... and take an active and equal role in partnership with other agencies" (2000, p 2). For them, the process includes aspects of training, consultancy, organisational and personal development, mentoring and peer group support. But the term must be used with care, however. Local people might, for example, find the implicit assumption that they need to increase their 'capacity' insulting or patronising. All too often, the assumption is that local people lack the wherewithal to deal with the 'complexities' of the regeneration process. As Henderson and Mayo note, "to imply that local people are 'empty vessels' simply waiting to be filled via training/capacity building ignores the wealth of existing knowledge and skills within communities" (1998, p v).

On the other hand, the term acknowledges the very real **power relationship** that exists between professionals and residents and the need to ensure that local people are in a position to take as much control as they wish, and are equipped with the knowledge and skills to do so. This is not, however, a simple and straightforward process. Some residents may have had years of experience of community action but others may be entirely new to the exercise, or have previously been excluded as a result of institutional racism and/or discrimination on the basis of gender. Unless capacity building actually begins to challenge these power relationships then exclusion will continue.

Power, it has been suggested, is not something that can be given to someone but rather something which is created by people when they "act collectively to transform their world" (Freire, 1970). If this is accepted, it follows that a long-term commitment is needed to facilitate a process that enables local people to work through their understanding of the problems they face and develop and implement the programmes they see as necessary. It should also be recognised that capacity building is futile without the associated **cultural changes** that are required within regeneration agencies, local authorities and those funding regeneration (Silburn et al, 1999; Duncan and Thomas, 2000; Taylor, 2000).

Barriers to effective community involvement

Research for the Foundation has shown that, despite the rhetoric,

> the impact of community involvement on regeneration has generally been modest and that commitment to community involvement has often been tokenistic. (JRF, 1999)

When challenged about the lack of involvement, regeneration professionals will often argue that they tried but that there was no interest – local people, it is claimed, are apathetic: they do not attend consultation meetings and, if they do, have little or nothing to contribute. Two factors are invariably overlooked: the **life experiences** that cause disaffection, including previous examples of inadequate consultation, and a whole range of **practical barriers** that prevent local people from getting involved or obfuscate those that do.

The previous life experiences of residents on low incomes in marginalised localities serve to reinforce low self-opinions and lead to feelings of inferiority and powerlessness. They are stigmatised simply because they live in areas with a poor reputation and it is often their perception that this leads to direct discrimination in relation to employment and in the receipt of mainstream services (Wood and Vamplew, 1999). Everything around them suggests that they are losers in a society where others are winning; *others*, they feel, do not listen to *them*. The emotional impact of these experiences should not be underestimated. Richard Wilkinson describes how the psychosocial effects of the feelings of failure lead to apathy, withdrawal, depression and aggression (1994). Given the harsh reality of their experience it is remarkable, and a testament to individual strength, that so many residents in these localities become actively and voluntarily involved in the affairs of their neighbourhood. However, considerable amounts of time and resources are often needed to allow participants to develop skills and gain the confidence that they require to believe in themselves. One of the clearest messages coming out of the ARP is that this has not occurred.

Insofar as resources are concerned, the findings suggest that while there are a range of agencies that support 'capacity building', provision is "neither comprehensive nor well coordinated" (JRF, 2000a, p 1) and that community groups are often bewildered by the burgeoning array of nationally-driven programmes (Duncan and Thomas, 2000). Particular gaps need to be filled quickly. There is currently no existing provision for the cost of involving local people in the preparation of Single Regeneration Budget (SRB) bids and, for those communities ineligible for SRB or New Deal for Communities, serious difficulties are often encountered when trying to secure relatively small amounts of money to facilitate community involvement. Many activists are 'out of pocket' because there are no funds to cover the cost of telephone calls, travel and basic administration. Consequently, residents and community workers often spend disproportionate amounts of their time fundraising for these activities. Duncan and Thomas conclude, from observations such as these, that:

- funding should be targeted at community groups;
- application procedures should be simplified;
- a Neighbourhood Empowerment Fund should be established to enable local communities to 'articulate their own priorities for regeneration' at the earliest possible stage in the process.

Their emphasis on involving local people right from the start is another dominant theme within the ARP. If communities are excluded at the beginning of regeneration programmes then there is a serious danger that the wrong issues will be prioritised and resources misdirected or wasted. Gaining meaningful involvement at a later stage would then be almost impossible. It is also common knowledge that early successes are essential to maintain community involvement in the long term:

> In communities that have been marginalised for many years, the confidence of local residents will often be at a low ebb and they may well be angry and frustrated. At an early stage, it can be helpful to encourage the community to take on some modest tangible projects that meet local needs. (JRF, 1999, p 2)

The boost that results from early successes can carry a community group through the difficult early months. It is also during this period that intensive training and support is required. Community development approaches, which start by working with people to identify what they believe to be the problems or issues that need tackling, are clearly fundamental.

Subsequent barriers to the inclusion of local people are often the result of an ignorance of or a lack of commitment to equal opportunities. Often, people are denied access at a basic level because little or no attention is paid to the accessibility of the venue and the timing of meetings. Even where childcare, transport and interpretation services *are* provided (which is the exception rather than the rule), more subtle barriers to participation may result from the formality of the proceedings and the 'exclusive' nature of the language used. In particular, a series of neighbourhood studies conducted as part of the ARP highlighted problems associated with representative structures:

- people were suspicious of them;
- some felt excluded from forums – they were said to be dominated by cliques;
- there was little knowledge about community representatives;
- there was little experience of consultation by the representatives with the wider community.

In summary, these structures "have not achieved a sense of power or inclusion for less involved residents" (Forrest and Kearns, 1999). Clearly, there is an imbalance in power, and "resources and the rules of the game" are controlled by the authorities (Taylor, 2000).

Research evidence suggests, for example, that "partnerships and other regeneration agencies typically failed to involve fully all sections of the population" and "many guidelines and evaluations [fail] to consider race and gender" (Brownill and Darke, 1998). The diversity of disadvantaged areas should be acknowledged and efforts made to ensure that the various perspectives that exist in an area are heard.

> Many of the activists in regeneration areas are women, but the significance of this is rarely analysed, neither is its impact on relations with partner agencies whose representatives are mostly male. (Brownill and Darke, 1998)

Such criticisms have led to the suggestion that the level of community participation in area regeneration programmes should be consistently evaluated. Danny Burns and Marilyn Taylor have developed a series of audit tools aimed at providing a 'health check' on the level of community participation (Burns and Taylor, 2000). These tools provide a means of mapping:

- the context for participation;
- the quality of participation structures;
- the capacity of partners and communities to participate;
- the overall impact of their participation.

Tools of this nature are currently being tested by two Regional Development Agencies.

Even where regeneration agencies and local authorities have a strong commitment to community involvement the short-term nature of many of the initiatives militates against genuine inclusion.

> The timescale of projects means that lead partners must quickly gear up to deliver their contracted outputs, rather than studying the area in detail or consulting widely on priorities before bids are drawn up. (Brownill and Darke, 1998)

A strong message emerging from the ARP is that the experience of exclusion and marginalisation in some areas is rooted in the local history. These places have faced stigma and discrimination, in some instances for many years; it will take many years to begin to repair the damage. As Taylor has pointed out:

> ... if adequate time is not allowed, commitment only runs skin-deep in statutory authorities while community involvement is confined to those already

known to public bodies – the 'usual suspects' – who can hit the ground running. (Taylor, 2000, p 9)

This tendency to recruit the same faces can lead to serious tensions within a neighbourhood. One neighbourhood study suggested that those who are involved may feel the burden – 'it's always left to the committed few' – and those who are not may feel debarred from involvement by an unrepresentative 'clique' (Wood and Vamplew, 1999).

Overcoming the barriers

Community development emerges, from the studies reviewed here, as the most significant factor in ensuring the genuine involvement of the community in regeneration. In a report synthesising the ARP neighbourhood studies, Ray Forrest and Ade Kearns state, "a community development approach can help foster supportive networks and relationships of trust" (1999). Duncan and Thomas describe the primary tasks for community development workers in the regeneration process as working with the community to:

> ... identify priorities, develop a community vision or plan, establish consultative and participatory structures and implement a comprehensive programme of support and resources for community-based activity and projects through a capacity building plan. (2000, p 29)

This is a process that requires:

- considerable experience of facilitating group development;
- a strong commitment to equal opportunities and anti-discriminatory practice;
- high levels of inter-personal skills;
- an ability to support and encourage learning;
- a good understanding of local government policy and practice;
- a keen political awareness.

Good training is essential and employers need to ensure that workers are given high levels of post-qualification support and the opportunity to progress within the discipline. This means that managers and managing bodies need to be familiar with the principles of community

development. Unfortunately, as Duncan and Thomas note, the trajectory is the other way and the 'profession' appears to have declined.

> Community development workers are often the main link a community has with programmes, funding and decision-making structures, but they are in increasingly short supply. Those that remain are often compromised by being employees of the agencies leading the programmes, usually local authorities. They rarely have enough status, senior management backing or access to infrastructure support, such as funding, financial advice and administrative assistance.... Community development is too often seen as a discretionary function and is vulnerable to cuts. Its long-term, non-output driven approach does not sit easily with the world of performance indicators and value for money. (Duncan and Thomas, 2000, p 10).

Certainly, since the focus of regeneration slipped away from neighbourhoods in the 1990s, there appears to have been an absolute reduction in the number of workers, a blurring of roles and general lack of understanding about the nature of the discipline. The current levels of competency among workers and their managers is questionable and needs to be evaluated carefully. Efforts need to be made to ensure that experienced and effective workers are retained by increasing status, improving remuneration and ensuring adequate career development options.

While the decline in community work should be of serious concern to those committed to community involvement, there are grounds for optimism. There has, for example, been a renewed emphasis on this approach as a strategy within 'neighbourhood management' and there is a clear opportunity for a renaissance of the approach. Taylor stresses, for example, the need for adequate 'high-status' community development posts to ensure "an active community with an informed constituency" (Taylor, 2000) and other studies have described how central "local representative structures *with community development support*" are to the process of community involvement (JRF, 1998, emphasis added).

Training for community involvement

Training is central to the process of involving communities in regeneration and is often what people are referring to when they talk about capacity building. But it is not just local people that require training. It is equally, if not more, essential for policy makers and regeneration professionals. Many of the topics that need to be covered in training programmes are common to all parties and there is a strong argument for **joint training**, but care needs to be taken to ensure that community groups have the space to identify their specific training needs. Henderson and Mayo, for example, refer to the need for provision to be rooted in the adult education tradition, where opportunities to learn start from a community's definition of their needs and where space is allowed for "critical reflection and political education for citizenship" (1998). They also note the lack of provision targeted at oppressed groups such as women, disabled people and ethnic minorities. There are, historically, strong links between informal learning strategies with oppressed groups (derived from the seminal work of Paulo Freire) and the community development process. It is important that this tradition is tapped, before reinventing the proverbial wheel, but it is also necessary to ensure that training is up-to-date and relevant.

Insofar as regeneration professionals and policy makers are concerned, the studies reviewed here suggest that training should primarily facilitate a **change in organisational culture and management style**: it is not necessarily new knowledge that is required but rather that attitudes and values change. What is needed is a shift from a 'we know best' culture to one that genuinely accepts the need to listen. As Henderson and Mayo put it, "the most crucial expertise of all [is] genuine understanding and respect" (1998).

Attention should be paid, however, to the process of training those who might facilitate this process and giving accreditation to this learning. In particular, opportunities should be provided for local people to gain qualifications through their experience and the opportunities to find employment in the regeneration 'industry'. In England, the Community Work Standards Board has developed occupational standards at NVQ levels 2 and 3 and regional organisations, such as the Community Work Training Company in West Yorkshire and the Community Work Accreditation Network for North East England, are exploring how SRB resources can be used to provide accredited training (JRF, 1999). There still appear to be gaps in the availability of higher education and professional development at post-qualifying levels – especially for community activists and professionals moving from other disciplines. A national centre for renewal along the lines of that proposed by the SEU's Priority Action Team 16 would be a welcome addition (SEU, 2000a).

Neighbourhood management

The new neighbourhood management proposals (SEU, 1998, 2000b) present exciting opportunities for community involvement in regeneration. The SEU's Priority Action Team 4 (Neighbourhood Management) report (SEU, 2000c) distils four main ingredients:

- someone in charge at neighbourhood level;
- reorganised public services as the main instrument of renewal;
- maximum involvement from communities and voluntary and private organisations;
- targeted assistance from government (Taylor, 2000).

In her review of existing models, Taylor identifies two approaches: those that are service-led or top-down, such as area coordination initiatives which 'join up' services at a local level; and those that are community-led or bottom-up. Examples of the latter include Tenant Management Organisations (TMOs) (see p 32) and the more recent development of Resident Services Organisations. Taylor argues that the two approaches do not need to be mutually exclusive and that "the most effective action is likely to come from strategies which engage effectively at all levels and are able to combine 'top-down' and 'bottom-up' forces for change" (2000, p 39). However, there is a clear tension between having 'someone in charge' and the principle of community involvement. There needs to be a clear understanding of where the power should lie, and decisions need to be taken by the community about the level of involvement they desire.

Taylor argues that "local residents do not always want to run their own services – any more than the rest of us", but asserts that they do wish to have a say (2000). This raises the question: do you need to run your own services to be in control? Clearly, this is not so. It appears, for example, to be the experience of the affluent that they may retain control over the services they receive without 'running' them. Crucially they can get things done or can change policies, if they wish, by exercising financial, legal or political control. How might this privilege be afforded to those on low incomes living in marginalised neighbourhoods? Does having someone in charge who can 'get things done' on their behalf empower local people or make them further dependent on others? Would it not be more 'empowering' to have a responsible individual who is answerable to the local community? Having a neighbourhood manager might improve service delivery but only if he or she is led by the community.

Service-led models, such as area coordination initiatives are characterised by the 'joining up' of council services at a neighbourhood level. In this approach, multi-disciplinary teams report to community forums or local area committees comprising local councillors. Other examples include the 'service development initiatives' introduced by housing associations normally known as 'housing plus'. Similar opportunities are opening up through Health and Education Action Zones and Sure Start (JRF, 2000). However, projects that are purely 'service led' will only succeed if they quickly become responsive to the community perspective.

Remarkably, many community groups do opt to run services themselves. Arguably, this is because local services are highly significant in situations where households cannot afford to meet their needs elsewhere: mutual support and collective action is often something that occurs out of necessity. Community workers can build on these initiatives and facilitate a process of empowerment. **Community-led initiatives**, such as TMOs, are clear examples of this.

There are two established forms of TMOs and these present a wide range of possibilities. Legislation, contained within the 1975 Housing Rents and Subsidies Act, allows local authorities to delegate the management of estates to **Tenant Management Cooperatives** (TMCs). These cooperatives are independent bodies and are controlled by tenants. Under a management agreement with the landlord, they take on responsibility for a range of functions, such as the allocation of property, day-to-day repairs, cyclical maintenance and environmental works. They are allocated a budget based on a management and maintenance allowance to fulfil this role. They often employ their own staff but may choose to undertake these roles themselves. TMCs may be governed by a committee elected from the membership but smaller cooperatives take all decisions to general meetings. This is only possible, however, because cooperatives rarely take on responsibility for more than 100 properties. **Estate Management Boards** (EMBs) are similar to TMCs but manage larger estates. Tenants on an estate may become members of a registered association; elected representatives from this association form a majority on a board which normally also includes local councillors and co-optees. Although general meetings are held for members of the association, decisions are made by the board (Phillips, 1992; Scott et al, 1994; Wood, 1994, 1996).

It is perhaps of significance that these models were developed within the sphere of housing management given that it is now fashionable to criticise regeneration initiatives with a strong housing bent. This tendency has resulted from an overemphasis on 'bricks and mortar' regeneration in the early 1980s, but the ARP neighbourhood studies suggest that the state of housing in a locality remains an important barometer for local people. Confidence in an area is sorely affected by the state of the physical infrastructure, layout and design, and the presence of empty housing (Cattell and Evans, 1999; Wood and Vamplew, 1999) and local people also recognise the significant impact that housing improvements have on the 'image' of the locality (Anderson et al, 1999).

TMOs have succeeded because local people are motivated by the tangible benefits of housing improvements. While educational and local economic development initiatives are clearly critical, their benefits are less apparent at the neighbourhood level (Maclennan, 2000). Housing investment should therefore retain its position as a central part of area regeneration while acknowledging the need for integrated responses. TMOs such as the Bloomsbury EMB, began by tackling housing issues but moved on to developing a credit union, a community café and a LETS (Taylor, 2000).

The principles contained within TMO arrangements have also been extended to other services in **Estate Agreements** (although not at such a high level of participation). These initiatives represent something of a halfway house between service-led and community-led initiatives. An Estate Agreement adopted on an estate in York, for example, includes:

> separate service-level agreements for community policing, street and environmental cleaning, jobs and training, leisure services, social services, housing, a dog warden service, the local adventure playground and the community education service. (JRF, 1998, p 4)

If the intention is genuinely to allow local people to 'own' or 'lead' local renewal efforts (SEU, 2000b) then it is **Resident Services Organisations** – where the management of services and appropriate budgets are devolved to resident controlled bodies – that should be considered (Saunders, 1997; JRF, 1998). While the TMO models are tried and tested they should not be imposed. Rather, interventions should facilitate a process of collective empowerment that might lead to the development of these types of structures. Experience suggests that the best TMOs have emerged after careful and sustained periods of community development work. The kind of community development interventions referred to above are therefore essential, and particular care should be exercised to ensure that local people are allowed to be in charge of the process from the earliest stage possible. This is important because, as Taylor notes:

> Neighbourhood Management is not simply to address the immediate problems that governments and communities identify, important though this is. It is: to ensure the economic, social and political inclusion of disadvantaged areas and their residents, so that they have access to their full rights as citizens. (Taylor, 2000)

Joblessness and inequality

However, it is also well recognised that the improved management of neighbourhoods will ultimately only succeed if the underlying problems of joblessness and inequality are also tackled. The lack of jobs was a major concern in all of the ARP neighbourhood studies and, while many of the regeneration initiatives operating in these localities had included strategies aimed at reducing unemployment, local people often remained cynical. Where attempts had been made to attract new jobs into the nearby or surrounding area, residents were "cautious or realistic about the prospects for local employment gain" (Forrest and Kearns, 1999) and there was an awareness that:

- jobs would go to others;
- such jobs might not last;
- people from their neighbourhoods still lack many of the skills sought.

Most local economic development initiatives have been focused on vocational training and improving job-search skills, but evidence suggests that the benefits are limited. For example, Mike Campbell has argued that, while such training played a role in securing employment for approximately 25% of the client group, they did not fundamentally change their overall employment prospects (Campbell, 1999). An earlier study suggested that where labour market interventions have been effective, the result has been that "capable residents leave poorer neighbourhoods" (McGregor and Maclennan, 1992).

In contrast, there has been a growing focus on how 'local demand' can be met locally and, while this may do little to change the overall scale of inequality, it is perhaps more relevant to what can be achieved at the neighbourhood level. For example, Richard Macfarlane argued that self-help and mutual aid could complement job creation as additional tools for tackling social exclusion (Macfarlane, 1997). This avenue has been further explored by Colin Williams and Jan Windebank (1999) who conclude that further policies are needed to help people do more for themselves and others. This includes:

- **'bottom-up' initiatives**, such as LETS, employee mutuals and mutual aid contracts, to tackle the lack of individual skills;
- new **'top-down' initiatives**, including reform of the 'voluntary and community sector' of New Deal for Communities and the introduction of an Active Citizens' Credits Scheme, to tackle issues related to benefit entitlement and social exclusion at the community level.

Beyond this, attention needs to be given to the levels of benefit paid to those out of employment. The JRF *Inquiry into income and wealth, inter alia*, highlighted the need:

- to redress the increasing inequality that has resulted from 'price indexation', by increasing benefits at times when living standards in general are rising;
- to ensure that more payments from the Social Fund should take the form of grants ... to allow long-term benefit recipients to replace household goods as they wear out. (JRF, 1995)

Good neighbourhood management is contingent on high levels of community involvement, but local residents can only fully engage when they have more control over their lives. This means redistributing wealth as well as power.

Levels of involvement

So far, this review has restricted the discussion of community involvement to the level of the neighbourhood, but local action alone will not tackle regional and national problems. Taylor's work suggests that the 'building blocks for change' need to include intervention at neighbourhood, district, regional and national levels and it is anticipated that regional or national networks of community organisations will be required to facilitate community involvement at all spatial levels (Taylor, 2000). **Community plans**, for example, present an opportunity for disparate community groups to network and identify common regeneration goals across districts and cities. **Regional Development Agencies** could fulfil a significant role in supporting the growth of local and regional networks and, as Taylor argues, "these could in turn be linked into a national forum for exchange" (2000).

In a report charting the evolution of regeneration policy, Stephen Hall and John Mawson explored the coordination of local initiatives (1999). As part of this study they reviewed the French *Contrats de ville* which produce a legally binding local regeneration strategy. This approach, they suggest, represents a "continuum from neighbourhood regeneration schemes to a National Plan via city-wide strategies and regional plans", and places more emphasis on the development of relationships than on achieving immediate result.

Overcoming social exclusion: key recommendations

Community involvement emerges as central to the process of empowerment and a necessary condition for overcoming social exclusion. If the barriers which prevent low-income households in marginalised neighbourhoods from engaging in action around locally identified issues are not removed there will be no inclusion.

Many of the barriers explored in the ARP can be tackled at the local level, and particular attention should be given to learning the lessons about the exclusion of residents from local partnerships:

- Community development is central to the process of involving people at this level and a renaissance of this approach will be essential if genuine involvement is to occur.

- Additional resources for community groups, such as the proposed Neighbourhood Empowerment Fund (Duncan and Thomas, 2000) should be established.

- Audit tools (see Burns and Taylor, 2000) should be used to evaluate community participation.

- Neighbourhood management can only come alive for residents if community development is moved up the agenda. The evolution of TMOs into Resident Services Organisations demonstrates the potential.

- Further policies are also required to support self-help and mutual aid initiatives such as LETS.

However, while local interventions of this nature are essential, the causes of inequality and social exclusion may be derived from regional, national and even international socioeconomic structures. Local solutions will only succeed if they work in tandem with regional and national policy. The government's commitment to reviving local economies (SEU, 2000b) should therefore be welcomed. Tackling joblessness is clearly essential if the inequities of inequality are to be challenged, but this will take time. Are other methods of redistribution required to ensure that neighbourhoods do not sink in the meantime?

3

Regeneration and employment

Mike Campbell

Summary
- Variations in joblessness are extensive and require a local dimension in policy design and delivery to effectively tackle the problem

- Joblessness in many deprived communities is a function both of a lack of jobs and difficulties in accessing existing job opportunities, within and around, such communities

- The prospects for effective local action could be improved by adherence to a range of policy design and implementation features

- Self-help activities are useful complementary tools to those that encourage paid employment

- The role of employers is crucial in taking effective action

- The needs of ethnic minorities should be explicitly taken into account in policy design and delivery

Policy implications
- The local policy mix needs to 'match' the specificity of local problems and labour market conditions

- Effective joined-up action and partnership working is central to success

- Community-based organisations could play a substantial role in policy and delivery

- Local Employment Plans need to be developed to give coherence to local actions on employment

Introduction

This chapter seeks to pull together the main findings of the range of Joseph Rowntree Foundation studies in its ARP which shed light on employment issues. The key themes are identified and the main lessons drawn. It is hoped that this may influence the policy and practice communities and help make their actions more effective as well as contributing to the development of a national framework for area regeneration. It is hoped therefore that local authorities, SRB partnerships and RDAs, in particular, will be interested in the findings.

However, this chapter is also relevant to a range of other organisations that 'connect' to the employment agenda including: Learning and Skills Councils, Connexions Services and Lifelong Learning Partnerships. It is also to be hoped that the main national organisations concerned with the employment and regeneration agenda – the DETR, DfEE and the Employment Service – will also be interested in the main findings.

This examination of employment issues arising from the ARP should be complemented by a reading of our assessment of the local dimension of the Work and Opportunity Programme which appears elsewhere (Campbell and Meadows, 2000).

The chapter proceeds as follows:

- first, the importance and meaning of the 'local' level in employment policy is outlined; second, brief consideration is given to the policy implications of the main analysis of employment undertaken under the ARP;
- third, evidence is reviewed on the effectiveness of various actions that have been undertaken;
- fourth, a number of 'alternative' approaches are explored;
- fifth, an outline is provided of the role of agencies in local employment;
- finally a set of conclusions are provided.

The importance of the 'local' level

The local dimension of employment policy is crucial in taking action to regenerate deprived communities because: joblessness is at the root of many social problems; local design and implementation adds value to policy; employment

policy is, in any case, decentralising and, empirically, there exists very substantial differences in labour market conditions across localities.

Certainly, the local dimension of employment policy and action is now seen as a crucial component of regenerating deprived communities. However, the term 'local', like the term 'area', is often used in an imprecise way. On occasion it can mean any 'level' beneath that of the region, a term which is itself open to interpretation. It is important to distinguish, therefore, at least in a UK context, between three levels. The first, is what some call the 'sub-regional' level. This, depending on population size, density and geographical coherence, may be a county (such as Hampshire), a group of counties (such as Devon and Cornwall) or a large conurbation or metropolitan area (such as West Yorkshire or Merseyside). Many Learning and Skills Councils and Connexion Services are configured at this level and many travel-to-work areas approximate to this level. Second, there is the local authority district level (such as, Southampton, Plymouth, Leeds or Liverpool respectively, in relation to the sub-regions identified above), which often is, or is based around, a town, city or group of towns. Third, there is the neighbourhood level – a small area within a local authority area – which may be a ward, group of wards, housing estate or other acknowledged 'community'. Such areas may have 'fuzzy' boundaries which can often be defined by reference to local knowledge and conditions, rather than by statistical artifacts or structures of local governance. This chapter will use the term 'territorial' when referring generally to those levels, and use the more precise terms – 'sub-regional', 'local' and 'neighbourhood' – as appropriate, when a particular level is being referred to.

The most important issue here is that different forms of local action for employment may be more appropriately carried out at one of these levels rather than another. There are at least four respects in which the 'territorial' level of employment policy is seen to be important.

First, joblessness is often seen as "lying at the root of many social problems in disadvantaged neighbourhoods" (Forrest and Kearns 1999). The National Strategy for Neighbourhood Renewal (SEU, 1998), for example, recognises that the main driver of 'neighbourhood decay' has often been economic, with 'mass unemployment' and the closure of particular industries 'devastating' communities, with new jobs requiring higher level skills and not enough help being available for people to adjust to the changing jobs market. Poverty and unemployment are also seen as exacerbating a whole range of social problems including ill health, youth disaffection, crime and family breakdown (SEU, 2000b). Thus, the National Strategy gives 'pole position' to its 'reviving economies' theme and, within this, there is a strong orientation to skills development, access to employment opportunities and business development.

Second, local approaches are increasingly seen as a more effective approach to the design and implementation of employment policies. Action at the local local level can add value to national policies in a range of ways (Campbell et al, 1998; OECD, 1998, 1999). It enables the adaptation of policy and practice to local conditions; it stimulates the involvement of a wide group of stakeholders, including employers and the local community; it makes intelligent use of local resources in terms of local accumulated knowledge and the 'social capital' of trust relations, proximity and communications, and team work; and it enables a 'joined-up' partnership-based approach to employment issues.

Third, much existing policy in relation to employment, and in its role in regeneration, is decentralising and localising. For example, the SRB programme involves substantial local design with local partnerships being responsible for developing their own strategies; the New Deal for Communities initiative involves local partnerships developing a flexible delivery plan utilising a 'bloc' grant available through Government Offices; both Employment Zones and the Action Teams for Jobs have substantial local discretion in designing 'what works' at the local level.

Finally, there is substantial local differentiation in labour market conditions across the country. For example:

- 65 local authority districts have a claimant unemployment rate which is more than double the national average;
- 37% of the long-term unemployed live in just 10% of local authority districts;

- 15 local authority districts have employment rates more than 10% below the national average;
- unemployment rates in the 100 'worst' wards in the country are over 15% points above the national average (Campbell and Meadows, 2000).

What's the problem?

Clearly there are substantial concentrations of employment disadvantage. However, two studies in the Area Regeneration Programme (Green and Owen, 1998; Turok and Edge, 1999) provide more detailed insights into the extent and nature of the problems; an understanding which is crucial if we are to devise appropriate measures to tackle the problems. These studies are outlined in Chapter 1, but a number of issues are also important in relation to their implications for territorial employment policy.

Green and Owen (1998) focus on the changing variations between, and within, urban areas in unemployment and non employment. They find that both local and regional inequalities in non-employment are greater than for unemployment especially in inner-city and former mining or industrial areas. Between 1981 and 1991, increased non-employment in many mining/industrial areas was due entirely to increased inactivity and not to unemployment. Moreover, the growth in both non-employment and inactivity was greatest where their initial incidence was highest – in inner cities and peripheral housing estates. They also point to the overall 'jobs deficits' (aggregate excess supply of labour irrespective of mismatch) which exist in some areas.

Critical to understanding the nature of these changes are the skills (who) and spatial (where) mismatches that have developed. Major changes in economic structure, occupational composition and their locations, have generated mismatches between the demand and supply sides of the labour market.

The crucial insight of this work is that 'conventional' unemployment only measures part of the joblessness problem. Non-employment is the issue and it comprises both unemployment and inactivity.

This focus on non-employment/inactivity is an issue taken up by the Jobs Policy Action Team report (DfEE, 2000a) which recommends that pilots be established to offer the New Deal service to all jobless people – irrespective of duration of unemployment or benefit claimed. It is also an issue addressed by the new Action Teams for Jobs which began work in the Autumn of 2000, where there is a strong focus on bringing the economically inactive back into employment.

Turok and Edge (1999) also draw attention to widening geographical disparities in labour market conditions in their examination of employment trends in 20 city regions. These cities experienced a loss of jobs between 1981 and 1996, while the rest of the country experienced a growth of 1.7 million jobs. While services have grown less slowly in the cities, declining manufacturing employment is largely responsible for the overall job loss – especially among full-time, male manual workers. However, there is substantial geographical unevenness in the experiences of different cities, conurbations and free-standing cities. Like Green and Owen, they argue that much of the growth in joblessness takes the form of 'hidden' unemployment, and that the heavy loss of jobs has been accompanied by declining economic activity and outmigration, thus masking the extent of the problem as rises in recorded unemployment are relatively small.

They also argue that the 'jobs gap' in these cities (the growing imbalance between the supply and demand for labour) is essentially caused by a lack of job opportunities, that is, an inadequate demand for labour.

These two pieces of work are based, in part, on the period 1981-91 and, in part, on 1991-96. More work needs to be done in this field to cover the late 1990s to assess the veracity of their findings in a period of strong overall employment growth as experienced from 1993 to date (see, however, Beatty and Forthergill, 1999, on inactivity).

In policy terms, Green and Owen argue for the need to customise welfare-to-work policy and provide quality job opportunities for the long-term unemployed in areas of high non-employment and 'demand deficiency'. They also call for support for community involvement in economic development actions and a stronger integration of economic development and employment policies. Turok and Edge propose a series of measures designed to stimulate the demand for labour – investment in cities' physical fabric and infrastructure, making serviced land available, providing premises (for expanding firms and inward investment) and modernising and replacing old buildings – especially 'within reach' of poorer neighbourhoods. They argue that neither supply-side measures (for example, skills, job-search, employability actions) nor national economic growth will alone resolve the joblessness problem.

However, Campbell and Sanderson (developing the argument first introduced in Campbell et al, 1998) argue that jobs growth in localities is not a sufficient condition for tackling concentrations of long-term unemployment (2000). They show that jobs growth does not necessarily 'trickle down' to the long-term unemployed or economically inactive. Job 'rich' areas – where jobs have been growing quickly – do not necessarily perform any better than job 'poor' areas – where jobs have been growing slowly or even declining – in terms of getting the long-term unemployed into work. Jobs tend to go to the short-term (registered) unemployed, to commuters and to new labour market entrants (school, college and university graduates and women returners), and not to the inactive or long-term unemployed.

Thus, the existence of concentrations of unemployment/non-employment does not necessarily imply an overall lack of jobs – jobs may be 'available', but the jobs may be unsuitable in terms of skills and experience required; the unemployed may not consider them to offer appropriate opportunities; the jobs may be in the 'wrong' places; employers may prefer to recruit workers other than the long-term unemployed and so on. Thus, jobseekers will face difficulties obtaining work even if the overall demand for labour were numerically sufficient to employ them.

Moreover, jobseekers may obtain jobs even when there is a 'jobs gap', as they may be able to fill jobs that become available through normal labour turnover, or they may 'connect' to new employment opportunities outside their community or locality – particularly if their skills match the opportunities.

Policy implications

It is necessary, therefore, to tackle the barriers that prevent the 'structurally' unemployed from accessing labour market opportunity through, for example:

- improving skills and qualifications (most notably basic skills, life skills and core skills in most cases);
- tackling personal, health, housing and family problems;
- activating job-search;
- adapting employer recruitment practices;
- providing childcare and other family care facilities, *inter alia* (see Sanderson et al, 1999).

The recent report and evidence from the House of Commons Education and Employment Committee (HCEEC) provides more evidence and discussion of the jobs gap (HCEEC, 2000a, 2000b). Broadly they conclude 'in favour' of the deficient demand arguments, while, like Turok and Edge (1999), acknowledging that supply-side actions have a role to play. In particular they propose:

- a job guarantee scheme in high unemployment areas for those who cannot obtain employment;
- public sector job provision, including the development of local resident services (the subject of a forthcoming Joseph Rowntree Foundation report by Roger Saunders of PEP Ltd, also see Campbell, 2000a);
- the further development of Intermediate Labour Markets;
- local tax structures to attract investment;
- the devolution of employment policy.

On the other hand, the Jobs Policy Action Team (DfEE, 2000b) and HM Treasury (HM Treasury, 2000) argue in particular for supply-side measures to 'connect' the excluded to evolving labour market opportunities. Both point to the existence of employment 'hot spots' outside, but potentially accessible to, people in deprived neighbourhoods, a point made also by Forrest and Kearns (1999). This draws attention to the need to link neighbourhood renewal to developments in the wider local and sub-regional areas and tackle the isolation – in this case economic – of many deprived communities.

The important issue is the nature and efficacy of the policy mix. It may well vary in different areas as patterns of labour demand, supply and community employment histories and locations interplay to provide a degree of local specificity. In these circumstances, if we are to secure effective action to create more employment opportunities and to connect the unemployed and inactive to employment opportunity, it is essential that the 'particularities' of each locality are understood, needs assessed and actions aligned with them.

What works?

What actions are most likely to be effective in improving the labour market prospects of the unemployed? Three studies in the programme address various aspects of this issue:

- Sanderson et al (1999) provide case studies of seven local SRB schemes in Nottingham, Leeds, Halifax, Huddersfield, Liverpool and London to examine what seems to 'make a difference' to the prospects of job seekers. (This study complements their earlier report [Campbell et al, 1998] which reviewed the literature on local responses to long-term unemployment.)
- Macfarlane (2000a) explores the potential of using Planning Agreements to link new developments to employment opportunities for local residents.
- Oc et al (1997) study the business and support training provided for ethnic minorities in the 31 City Challenge areas in the mid-1990s.

The lessons provided here should be viewed in parallel with the lessons that can be learnt from those studies in the Work and Opportunity Programme which focused on the local level. These cannot be discussed here, but see Campbell and Meadows (2000) for a detailed account.

Towards effective local action

Sanderson et al (1999) find that, overall, the SRB schemes studied played a key role in obtaining employment for between a fifth and a quarter of their clients but did not appear to fundamentally change the overall employment prospects for their client group. Those most likely to be successful were women, those who were better qualified, those with limited previous experience of unemployment and those who were married with working partners. The least successful were those already most vulnerable – poorly qualified men, single parents with young children, and those with a history of previous unemployment. Those aged 16-19 and over 50 also generally received less attention than their circumstances merit.

The main lessons for designing schemes to meet the needs of the most disadvantaged are:

- A good understanding of the target client groups and their needs together with outreach work to encourage participation of 'hard-to-reach' groups.
- A client-focused, holistic approach to address the full range of circumstances, problems and barriers faced by individuals, including personal, financial and social as well as vocational factors. Thus provision should be tailored to individuals' specific needs designed to promote progression along 'pathways' to employment.
- Personalised 'casework' approach with action planning and ongoing support and review of progress including support for childcare and travel needs, and advice on benefits.
- Developing close working relationships with employers to secure work opportunities for clients and to ensure provision is relevant to their needs.
- Provision of a range of work experience options to build the confidence of clients in various circumstances (such as part-time and voluntary work)
- Ongoing monitoring of progress and support after achieving employment to ensure any problems with the transition to work are addressed.
- Training focused on the needs of individuals and employers, especially 'tailored' pre-recruitment packages and training linked to work experience placements.
- Effective and joint working and partnership at both strategic and operational levels between all relevant agencies, especially the Employment Service, local authorities, TECs and training providers.
- A strategic approach to management, with clear objectives and effective management practices and systems including monitoring and evaluation, underpinned by appropriate information systems.

It is important that these design features are incorporated in the development, delivery and management of local actions in the future.

Planning Agreements

Macfarlane's assessment of the potential for using Planning Agreements (the commitment by a developer to the Planning Authority in a legally binding form) to link new developments to local employment opportunities, provides a potential basis for action to link the growth of employment with access to those opportunities for local and/or disadvantaged groups (Macfarlane, 2000a; see also Macfarlane, 2000b). His work also covers four case studies whose Agreements have included employment-related clauses with seemingly strong positive effects in three: Southampton, Greenwich and Aberdeenshire. It raises the issue that planning and development control can be about more than land use issues and could be used as tools to address local employment priorities through 'targeted recruitment'. All new developments need approval, and local authorities (who are usually the relevant planning authority) are able to consider whether such an Agreement is appropriate. Currently only one in eight use relevant clauses in them, covering about 90 developments. Macfarlane estimates that this covers only 1-2% of the number of Agreements in any one year, although their use is more extensive in the London boroughs. The low level of their use is usually because planning officers do not consider development control powers as an instrument of local employment policy; because there is some uncertainty about the legal position; and possibly because they perceive such Agreements as a barrier to potential inward investors.

Macfarlane proposes that government should include such considerations when issuing planning guidance and argues that success in the use of Agreements is most likely when:

- they are used to provide a basis for ongoing cooperation with developers;
- the local authority makes clear its intentions in local plans and development briefs;
- the issue is focused on at an early stage in discussions with developers;
- there is joint working between development control and economic development staff.

Ethnic minority groups

Oc et al's work (1997) draws attention to the crucial issue of how ethnic minority groups fare in relation to employment and related issues in the regeneration process. One should note, however, that different ethnic minority groups are confronted by different issues. Oc and his colleagues examine ethnic minorities' access to training and business support in all 31 City Challenge areas that operated, under its two rounds of bids, from 1992-97. They reviewed all the action plans and undertook six case studies, interviewing providers and 600 clients. They found that recognition of the additional disadvantages that ethnic minorities face was patchy across the 31 areas with, in some cases, such recognition being 'marginal'. The issue was also not emphasised in DfEE guidance. For example, of the 23 core outputs, there were no specific ones relating to ethnic minorities.

They also found that effective delivery of training and business support was critically dependent on the relations of the City Challenge partnership to the local authority and local TEC and on the capacity of the voluntary and community sector in the area. Moreover, in themselves, they argue, higher skill levels and business support is insufficient to gain access to employment – other barriers need to be tackled. They demonstrate that the outcomes of training, for example, were not dissimilar between whites and the ethnic minorities. They propose that greater dialogue is necessary between agencies and the ethnic minority communities and that, given the additional barriers that they face, greater resources will be needed to achieve similar outputs and outcomes to other groups.

While City Challenge is no more, the issues raised are pertinent to the 'new' agencies which will soon be developing and delivering training and business support – the Learning and Skills Councils and the Small Business Service – as well as being relevant to regeneration initiatives such as SRB, New Deal for Communities and the Neighbourhood Renewal Fund. They are also relevant to locally-based or targeted employment policies, such as Employment Zones and New Deal.

It is worth noting that the Policy Action Teams had a remit to specifically examine disadvantaged ethnic minority groups, and many of their recommendation focus on that issue. For example, the Jobs PAT calls for "a concerted assault on racial discrimination in the labour market" (SEU, 2000d). Indeed, the SEU has published a brief guide to the ethnic minority aspects of the PAT reports.

The key recommendations for future policy and practice proposed by Oc and his colleagues thus deserve serious consideration:

- Regeneration policies should focus explicitly on the special needs of disadvantaged groups, such as ethnic minority groups, to enable them to compete better in the mainstream economy.
- Ethnic minority groups should be involved in programme design and delivery; local 'ownership' of training projects should be fostered.
- Ethnic minority groups are often less aware of the provision of training courses. Potential ethnic minority trainees must be made aware of the availability of training courses by appropriate means: for example, advertising in ethnic minority social centres, shops and places of worship. Personal recommendation through word-of-mouth is particularly important in many ethnic minority communities.
- Ethnic minorities experience greater cultural alienation from traditional environments. Training projects to benefit ethnic minority groups must both encourage and enable trainees to 'get through the door'. They should also reduce other barriers to participation in training, provide pastoral care and welfare support during training, and careers advice before, during and after training.
- Training programmes should be complemented by other initiatives that recognise and positively address the range of impediments to employment which include postcode and racial discrimination. Action to tackle the latter should include training on equal opportunities, employment and recruitment practices for local employers.
- Awareness of business support services must be enhanced among ethnic minority businesses. Equally, business support agencies frequently fail to engage sufficiently with ethnic minority businesses. They must therefore establish channels of communication both to individual firms and groups of firms, and foster networks of local ethnic minority businesses and/or all local businesses. Proactive outreach by business support advisers who are sufficiently sensitive to the needs of ethnic minority businesses is a means of both raising awareness and of establishing contact.

- Business support agencies must be demonstrably sensitive to ethnic minority business needs, problems and opportunities; focused business support strategies should enable ethnic minority businesses to 'break out' of co-ethnic markets. Assistance might include mentoring from ethnic minority businesses who have already broken out, advice on accessing new markets and the delegation of managerial authority.

Alternative and micro approaches

Self-help

Williams and Windebank (1999) examine the extent to which 'self-help', that is helping people to help themselves and each other, through household work, DIY, mutual aid (unpaid work) and informal exchange, could be developed as an extra tool to tackle social exclusion and complement job creation. They surveyed 400 households in four deprived areas in Southampton and Sheffield, to examine the extent of self-help activity and the barriers to people's participation in such 'work'. They argue that the importance of this approach lies both in the wide gulf between current conditions and 'full employment', especially in deprived areas, and in the way the UK is 'informalising', with people spending an increased amount of time on unpaid work. More specifically, they argue that in poor communities many households are unable to get basic tasks done, but that when they do, in more than 80% of cases, they use their own or friends', relatives' and neighbours' labour. People participate in self-help as a means of engaging in meaningful and productive activity as well as for social purposes and it is, more often than not, undertaken out of choice rather than necessity.

The barriers to increasing self-help include access to equipment, networks of people, skill levels and 'fear' of the social security system. Tackling these could stimulate self-help and move us towards a 'full engagement' rather than a full employment society, where self-help is recognised and valued. Williams and Windebank propose a number of 'complementary' policies, therefore, to those that target paid employment as the objective. These include:

- Local Exchange and Trading Schemes (LETS);
- Employee Mutuals (Leadbetter and Martin, 1998);

- Active Citizens Credits (where people undertake a portfolio of work and as recompense get 'hours' which they could spend by requesting hours in return).

In an interesting 'think piece', Macfarlane (1997) makes similar, although broader, proposals. Like Williams, he is skeptical about 'mainstream' approaches and proposes enhancing the well-being of the non-working population *either* as a temporary measure pending 'full employment' in deprived communities *or* as a pilot approach for the operation of a society where not everyone needs to work.

He argues that non-working people could be encouraged to improve their own 'household' economy. The approach is designed to work with four elements commonly used to 'get by' in poor households: state benefits; voluntary action; the informal economy; and collective self-help. He proposes means by which they could be made more effective, for example:

- increasing the earnings disregard;
- actively encouraging voluntary work and offering payment for it;
- extending the operation of intermediate labour market initiates (ILMs) in themselves and not necessarily as a route to other employment;
- supporting the growth of self-help through training and 'start up' assistance.

MacGillivray and his colleagues (2000) focus on 'informal community action' – the 'space' between family and friends and formal community or voluntary action – or what are called 'micro social enterprises' (MSEs). These 'low flying heroes', which thrive in adversity, are informal groups, usually motivated by social and environmental benefits, who are making a real (but often invisible to outsiders) contribution to social inclusion, neighbourhood renewal and more sustainable communities. These organisms of community self-help do not have staff, offices, funding and formal organisation but, they argue, they do have ideas, enthusiasm and the 'nous' to make things happen. They estimate that there may be between 600,000 and 900,000 informal actors, with anywhere between 1.8 and 5.4 million people involved in some way.

Based on a series of case studies using semi-structured interviews in Birmingham and Hastings, as well as three case studies of 'achievers' (formal voluntary organisations which were once MSEs), they conclude that, while MSEs are diverse in terms of motivation, ambition and dynamics, they generally require a range of assistance. This includes help with networking with like-minded groups, advice on managing the transition (if they want to) to something more formal or larger, access to facilities and premises, and, perhaps most important of all, a need to be 'recognised' by the statutory authorities.

These groups have the energy and commitment to assist with local renewal and are usually based on the important principle of mutuality and reciprocity, and thus of 'self-help' and 'mutual aid' (Taylor, 2000). These offer the prospect of a 'new mutualism' in communities which could add a new dimension to local development. The key ingredients for their success, it is suggested, include:

- *Inspiration:* having the idea, determination and obtaining recognition.
- *Resources:* volunteer time, equipment and space to meet.
- *Relations:* building connections within the 'sector' across localities, and building relations with public agencies.

The authors call on government to provide a 'non-profit' counterpart to the new Small Business Service, to reduce paperwork needed to access funding, and for SRB partnerships and the RDAs to "back MSEs to the hilt".

Policy

The Policy Action Team report on community self-help focuses on many of the issues raised in Williams, Macfarlane and MacGilivray's work. The report makes a series of recommendations to develop local self-help, including:

- the Active Community Unit of the Home Office should develop policy on volunteering and community involvement;
- modification of benefit rules;
- simpler financial reporting;
- increasing spending on community involvement in, for example, the various New Deals;
- increasing the recognition of the role of 'faith' communities.

This work on alternative and micro approaches draws attention to the need to broaden our view of the role of employment in regeneration, by ensuring that policy and practice takes account of forms of endeavour, engagement and gainful activity other than 'paid work'.

Organising for jobs

Studies of the various forms of self-help discussed above also raise the issue of 'agency'. That is to say, what are the most appropriate organisational forms to design and deliver employment action in localities. Three studies in the Area Regeneration Programme address aspects of this issue. Michael Ward (1997) examines the role of neighbourhood-based agencies, in particular, Community Development Trusts (CDTs), as a vehicle for tackling deprivation and exclusion in marginalised communities, through a review of the relevant literature, and an examination of the role of around 150 of these organisations, utilising a postal survey, seminars and consultations. Plummer and Zipfel (1998) assess the role of Training and Enterprise Councils (TECs) and Local Enterprise Councils (LECs) in regeneration in considering (1) whether they see the terrain in a narrow way which causes them to overlook social exclusion issues; and (2) the extent to which other organisations find it difficult to develop effective regeneration partnerships with TECs. Finally, Alan McGregor et al (1999) examine the role that employers can play in the employment agenda of regeneration and, critically, how their effectiveness could be increased. McGregor produced a directory of projects involving employers, based on telephone interviews together with the detailed evaluation of 12 of the projects through interviews and group discussions with project managers, funders, employers and former participants.

Community-based organisations

Michael Ward's study shows how most CDTs grew out of local initiatives or problems, and focus largely on tackling unemployment together with improving the 'quality of life' in deprived communities. They engage mainly in community development activity, training, environmental improvements and property 'development' on a small scale. Their distinctive role is in mobilising the active participation of local residents in regeneration – stimulating community involvement. However, they face two main problems. First, the short-term nature of their funding, which is also limited to specific projects.

This means that they usually lack working capital and have limited access to loans. Second, there is no appropriate legal form to their existence and activities. For CDTs to develop into sustainable organisations a number of developments are required:

- increased awareness among partners of their actual and potential role;
- a commitment from government and other agencies to their role and development;
- stronger networks and a coordinated 'voice';
- development finance and access to working capital so that they can build an asset base;
- training, technical support and other capacity building measures.

CDTs have continued to develop since this study was undertaken and government is increasingly involving community organisations in service delivery. The National Strategy for Neighbourhood Renewal recommends this involvement as well as forms of neighbourhood management which involve community organisations (on which also see SEU, 2000c).

TECs

Plummer and Zipfel (1998) assess the role of TECs and LECs in six areas, and the factors that determine success in regeneration partnerships. While TECs are being replaced by the new Learning and Skills Councils (LSCs) early in 2001, the issues examined remain relevant, as LSCs will want to work, like TECs, with local authorities, the Connexions Service, RDAs and others, to link their skills agenda to those of area regeneration and social inclusion. The issue of partnership and how such agencies engage with agendas some way 'removed' from their core fields, will be a major issue in the next few years and the lessons of this study will be of interest to LSCs in particular.

Plummer and Zipfel found that many TECs targeted deprived areas and sought to respond to their specific local needs, although it should be noted that the resulting agenda was not necessarily one of social inclusion. Attitudes to, and relations with, community and voluntary organisations varied, but were usually perceived as relatively unimportant in terms of participation in training and employment, and they only rarely involved clients or target groups in shaping and delivering programmes. Furthermore, self-help

organisations, cooperatives and community enterprises were rarely seen as eligible for start up assistance.

While, on formation, there was considerable distrust between TECs, local authorities and community organisations, evolving collaboration did increase TEC credibility and some (for example, Calderdale and Kirklees TEC and Glasgow Development Agency) took these issues very seriously. This is most important as the fragmentation of agencies, policies and implementation structures as well as the 'complexity' of employment actions themselves, necessitate 'joined-up' actions and solutions. Thus, partnerships provide the crucial glue needed to coordinate, to fill gaps and, above all, to provide a coherent framework within which action can take place. What influenced the development of effective partnerships? In the view of Plummer and Zipfel, motivation, identity (coterminous boundaries between TEC/LEC and local authority, as well as a common vision), a sound understanding of regeneration and the quality of relations with local government were key factors. Also important is mutual understanding and the development of trust.

Carley et al's study (2000, see Chapter 4) found that the key factors in determining partnership success were leadership, vision, clarity of objectives, the building of consensus, appropriate membership, high quality staff and an effective organisation. These are very similar to those identified by other authors (including Hutchinson and Campbell, 1998; Campbell, 2000a). Key recommendations include:

- broadening the base of partnerships;
- empowering the community;
- 'joining-up' thinking, policies and partnerships;
- the provision of a clear coherent regional and national framework within which to locate them.

This applies to the employment agenda as much as to other aspects of area regeneration.

Like TECs, the LSCs have an important and distinctive contribution to make to the local employment agenda, given the critical role of skills in enhancing employability and stimulating local jobs growth (Campbell, 2000c). Thus, it will be desirable for LSCs to, from the beginning, build in mechanisms to prioritise the needs of deprived areas and to develop effective partnership working (for example, guidance and workshops), and to develop broader competences in regeneration processes, including the social inclusion agenda and area-based working on the one hand, and locally-based employment initiatives on the other. Relations with the RDAs and Government Offices on territorial employment issues will be particularly crucial given the uncertainty and lack of clarity about the relations (Robson et al, 2000). For example, RDAs still currently have responsibility for the SRB, while Government Offices have responsibility for European Funds and New Deal for Communities (although this will change by 2002 under the proposals contained in the July 2000 Spending Review).

Engaging employers

Enhancing the role of employers in local action to get the unemployed back to work is the theme of Alan McGregor et al's important report (1999). Employers can be involved in a wide range of ways, including working with schools and colleges to enhance 'employability', job-taster and work experience provision, provision of customised training, interview coaching and guarantees, provision of subsidised employment opportunities and the provision of sustainable jobs in the community. Indeed, it is difficult to imagine successful local employment actions which do not effectively engage employers. What, then, are the key ingredients through which engagement can be increased? McGregor proposes the following template for local initiatives:

- Decide what role you want employers to play in implementing your regeneration strategy.
- Establish a single contact point for interested employers to approach, but go out and talk to them as well.
- Engage potentially important employers at an early stage in the process, and listen to their views.
- Invite employers to use their networks to widen the pool of participating employers.
- Put in place an 'account management' system where only one member of the initiative (and ideally the local partnership as a whole) deals with the employer.
- Help the employers access all the financial assistance that might be available for recruiting a particular category of client.

- Strive to generate direct benefits for participating employers to maintain their involvement.
- Explore the range of ways in which engaged employers can contribute.
- Where a relationship has been established with employers, discuss whether their recruitment practices act against the residents of regeneration areas and, if so, whether they might be changed.

One important assumption lies behind the contribution of employer involvement – that the key to tackling high unemployment in deprived communities is in the wider labour market and that 'access' to opportunities – outside the communities in most cases – is the critical success factor that will make the difference to the employment prospects of people in deprived communities. This is predicated, of course, on the actual existence of such opportunities in the areas around deprived neighborhoods. Employers need to play a direct role, involving them in projects, which, after all, seek to give local people access to 'their' jobs. As McGregor argues, "a straightforward equation between the creation of new local jobs and getting local, unemployed people back into employment cannot be assumed", as an extensive array of barriers stands between the unemployed and job opportunities. The linkage needs to be strengthened and, thus, the recruitment process and relations with employers move to the centre of local employment policy.

The 12 detailed studies, including those of Drumchapel Opportunities, Hartlepool Jobs Build and Leeds Job Placement, demonstrate, in concrete terms, the real value of employer engagement in a practical way. It should also be noted that public as well as private sector employers need to be involved and targeted (for example, hospitals, local authorities, government departments) as well as 'third sector' organisations who have a potentially significant role to play (Campbell, 1999). Getting business more involved in regeneration is one of the 'key ideas' of the National Strategy for Neighbourhood Renewal (SEU, 1998), as is connecting the unemployed to wider job opportunities (see also HM Treasury, 2000; DfEE, 2000b).

Concluding remarks

A noticeable feature of 'local' action for employment is that it is generally undertaken without there being a clear or consistent framework to guide it. The wide range of national programmes and the diversity of local action, in terms of both content and agency, have generated a jigsaw of area-based employment initiatives which are inadequately mapped, infrequently evaluated effectively, and wherein good practice is not always recognised, valued or transferred. Much remains to be done to develop an effective territorial dimension to employment policy (see, for example, Campbell and Meadows, 2000).

In this context, it would be valuable to develop a Local Employment Plan at three levels:

- First, as an organising framework **for action at the local authority level** – a strategic, comprehensive actions plan embedded within a local area's overall Community Plan.
- Second, the same framework could be used to inform **Neighbourhood Employment Plans** for deprived communities within the local area.
- Third, **national guidance** could be provided on the main dimensions of such plans, so that a degree of consistency was provided and local action was informed by good practice. Such a Local Employment Plan could have three key components:
  - *economic development and labour market opportunity:* generating jobs;
  - *enhancing employability:* helping people to acquire the aptitudes and skills required in the labour market;
  - *building bridges to work:* providing access to employment opportunity (see Campbell and Meadows, 2000, for more detail on Local Employment Plans).

The 'localisation' of employment policy is gathering pace as it is increasingly recognised that substantial local variations in labour market conditions are most effectively tackled by locally targeted, and increasingly locally designed, policies and actions. This chapter has drawn attention to a range of issues examined and identified through the Area Regeneration Programme, which would be valuable for local, regional and national agencies and partnerships to address in their search for more effective local action on joblessness.

The key issues

- It is important to distinguish the various meanings of 'local' and to acknowledge that different forms of action for employment are most appropriately carried out at different levels.

- Action should focus on the issue of joblessness *per se* – unemployment, inactivity and non-employment in general – rather than just on those people who are captured by the claimant count of unemployment and are in receipt of the Jobseekers' Allowance.

- The substantial 'jobs gap' in many deprived localities and communities is generally a function of both a lack of job opportunities and difficulties in accessing existing job opportunities.

- A more detailed understanding is required of the nature and causes of joblessness in specific localities before appropriate action can be designed and delivered.

- The local 'policy mix' needs to match the specific nature of the problems identified in the locality.

- Adherence to the full range of local options will enhance the prospects of effective local action.

- The needs of ethnic minorities should be taken into account explicitly in the design of local action.

- A range of self-help activities are also useful complementary tools to those designed to develop job opportunities in deprived communities.

- There is a substantial role to be played by community-based organisations in the design and delivery of local employment action.

- Statutory agencies need to work closely in partnership with each other and with the community if action is to be effective.

- The role of employers in local action for employment needs to be developed and sustained.

- There is a need to develop Local Employment Plans to provide a coherent approach to employment issues at the local level, perhaps most notably at the local authority level. These could be nested in local Community Plans drawn up by Local Strategic Partnerships and provide a basis for Neighbourhood Employment Plans.

4

Partnerships – realising the potential

Raymond Young

Summary

- A multi-agency approach is needed to tackle the interrelated issues that face communities in decline. To be properly effective partnerships need to genuinely involve the residents and ensure that they are able to play a role in reviving their neighbourhood; by identifying the priorities or by laying the foundations for long-term sustainable neighbourhood management

- Relationships are at the heart of urban regeneration partnerships – between residents and their council, and with other service providers, and between agencies themselves. Like all relationships, partnership must be worked at if it is to produce satisfactory outcomes; they involve sharing political power and need strong leadership to be effective – normally from the local authority.

- While the choice of partners is an important factor in the ultimate success of the partnership, equally important (if not more so) is the nature of their involvement. Spending time and energy getting the right stakeholders, building relationships and developing an inclusive vision based on community analysis will create a culture that will pay huge dividends later.

- Partnership structures and the styles of working have a dynamic relationship. Successful partnerships require the development of trust between partners, and the creation of a partnership culture. Conflict resolution processes are a priority. Training is needed for both professionals and residents.

- Short-life partnerships need to plan an exit or forward strategy including the creation of community organisations or neighbourhood management processes.

- Partnership perfection is difficult to achieve; indeed there is no perfect model. Partnerships will change, adapt and – hopefully – mature over time.

Policy implications

- More emphasis should be given to process, and to how relationships are developed within partnerships. Monitoring should reflect local needs and process.

- Partnerships need to be helped to streamline the bureaucracy involved with the bidding process, reporting and monitoring arrangements that emanate from different levels of government – local, central and European.

- More recognition should be given to the time required for the relationships to develop, and the impact that these relationships might have on the vision and the objectives.

- More recognition should be given to the power inequalities within partnerships and to how the inevitable conflicts can be resolved.

- Race, gender and youth inclusion should be regarded as strategic partnership issues. Those assessing partnerships should develop equal opportunity 'badging' to ensure that partnerships are operating inclusively.

- Funding should be available at the beginning of the partnership for training and capacity building for both the community and other partners.

- Local and national government should recognise that strategic objectives should be changeable to reflect community views and the role of the community.

Regeneration programmes in Britain are delivered through partnerships. Virtually every area or local regeneration project operates a local partnership; sometimes that partnership relates to a city- or region-wide partnership, and it may contain a number of other partnerships. It will often be part of health, New Deal, education, youth or other partnerships. There is no escaping partnership in Britain in the 21st century – the political style of the moment is partnership.

The government encourages partnerships, and the establishment of a partnership is an essential step in securing funds for regeneration, whether in England (SRB Challenge Fund), Scotland (Social Inclusion Partnerships and New Housing Partnerships) or Wales (Social Inclusion Fund and People in Communities Programme). It is part of the 'joined-up' government approach, requiring local authorities and public agencies to coordinate their activities and investment. But it is also – particularly at a local level – a way of involving residents in the decisions that affect their lives.

The draft National Strategy for Neighbourhood Renewal, published by the Social Exclusion Unit (SEU, 1998), recognises the importance of partnerships at both a local or neighbourhood level and at a city or regional level. It proposes **Local Strategic Partnerships** for England as the means of taking forward neighbourhood renewal and providing the link between region- and city-wide policies, on the one hand, and neighbourhood actions on the other. Partnerships are therefore viewed at a national policy level as the future key to regeneration processes.

Nearly all the ARP studies touch on partnership. One (Carley et al, 2000) studied the effectiveness of 27 partnerships in nine urban regions in England, Wales and Scotland. Others looked at the partnership process from the viewpoint of a local neighbourhood or of a community group. All of them identified good practice, bad practice and indifferent practice. They reinforce work that has been carried out in other research programmes – that, despite the large amount of good practice guides, 'do-it-yourself' manuals and organisations that specialise in helping partnerships develop, partnerships are not realising their potential. Although some are providing positive results, partnership working is still causing frustration, disillusionment and exclusion among many residents and professionals.

There are a number of key findings and recommendations that come out of the ARP studies. This chapter will concentrate on local or neighbourhood partnerships and look at four main issues:

- Why partnerships?
- Relationships are at the heart of partnerships.
- It's not just who you involve – it's the way that you do it.
- Realising the potential.

Why partnerships?

The current vogue for partnership working goes back many years. The concept is simple – working together towards a common goal. It reflects the reality of the causes of urban decline. As set out in Chapter 1, these are complex and interrelated:

- unemployment and non-employment;
- poverty;
- the feelings of social exclusion and entrapment felt by residents;
- low educational attainment;
- poor health;
- poor quality and poorly managed housing;
- area abandonment.

These are issues that cannot be tackled separately, nor tackled by any one agency alone. They require a multi-agency approach, and over the last 20 years many public agencies and local authorities have become used to working together in this way.

But multi-agency working is not enough. To be properly effective the residents need to be involved to ensure that they genuinely benefit from the regeneration activity, and are able to play a role in reviving their neighbourhood by identifying the priorities or to lay the foundations for long-term sustainable neighbourhood management.

So, partnerships are not just the result of the need for multi-agency work at a time when the powers of local authorities have been changed and they are no longer sole providers of services – if they ever were. It could be argued that one reason for regeneration programmes is that the traditional relationship between residents and their service providers (including their local authority) has broken down and a new one needs to be created. Partnership is seen as the way to do this – a working together of residents and service suppliers, a sharing of power between residents and government, and the creation of new forms of neighbourhood management and governance. In many cases this will include new community-based organisations, such as Community Development Trusts and new forms of housing ownership. Indeed, one of the key aims of some partnerships will be to transfer power and responsibility for basic services such as housing to the local community.

This is particularly true where earlier regeneration programmes are perceived by residents to have been ineffective, or, at best, cosmetic, leading to suspicion about the sincerity and commitment of the public authorities to genuine partnership where some power is devolved (Silburn et al, 1999).

The other reason for partnership working is that it is a funding requirement. Bennett et al (2000) have described the purpose of many partnerships as "to access funding in competition with other places ... they may reflect the eligibility of government funding regimes rather than the particular needs and aspirations of localities". This may change – at least within local authority areas in England – if Local Strategic Partnerships are involved in coordination at a local authority level. But, even if the reasons for setting up the partnership are sometimes reluctant, and sometimes opportunist, the process can be a positive force for change.

Relationships are at the heart of partnerships

At the heart of urban regeneration partnerships is the relationship between residents and their council, between residents and other service providers, and between agencies themselves. Regeneration is not simply a short term 'fix' for an area, but involves a long-term relationship change – one that encompasses the governance of the area and how the residents in that area relate to the wider city or regional community. For 'residents', read not only those who have their homes in the area, but those who work and play there or who, at a local level, have a contribution to make to the well-being of the area.

Leadership

Someone must take the lead in establishing a relationship and strong leadership plays a vital role in partnership success. Good leadership brings visibility to the partnership, promotes shared ownership of the agenda, can draw in reluctant partners and can drive forward a sometimes contentious regeneration agenda.

Normally, but not always, the local authority will take the lead. Certainly the local authority has to play a key strategic role. Carley et al (2000) found that the most effective partnerships are those with strong political and executive leadership at a most senior level. The commitment of council leaders and chief executives can make or break the partnership. They set the tone for the rest of the partnership, not just for their own colleagues – politicians and officials – but for the other agencies as well. If they do not take the partnership seriously, then it will fail. For many elected representatives and local authority officers, however, the style of working in a regeneration partnership is totally different to the political process that he or she is used to (Silburn et al, 1999). Partnership is not about control and group power; rather it is about sharing power, and that style may need to be developed through training.

Political and executive leadership go hand-in-hand. Managerial leadership can come from the local authority, or, as has successfully been the case in many area partnerships, from staff reporting to the partnership board, either on secondment from partners or appointed directly.

It's not just who you involve, but the way that you do it

All of the studies are clear that while the **choice of partners** is an important factor in the ultimate success of the partnership, equally important (if not more so) is the **nature of their involvement**. As with all good relationships, partnership has to be worked at if it is to produce satisfactory outcomes. The more successful partnerships will admit that it can be hard but rewarding work: spending time and energy getting the right stakeholders, building relationships and developing an inclusive vision based on community analysis will create a culture that will pay huge dividends later.

Choosing partners

Choosing the partners is the first stage. The more successful partnerships have carefully thought through who should be involved as stakeholders.

The **local community** is the most obvious partner but, in many ways, the most difficult to properly engage. Participation is fundamentally a political issue. Carley et al (with help from the Scottish Executive) developed a typology of partnership.

Typology of partnership

Consultation: securing the views of residents, for example by surveys, panels and juries.

Representation: community members on regeneration partnerships, including board membership.

Service involvement: in decision making about local service priorities and assessment of the quality of service. This is the level at which most neighbourhood management programmes operate.

Empowerment: where community and neighbourhood groups take their own decisions and control resources (and therefore take the responsibility for service delivery), for example, through development trusts or community based housing associations

Community representatives are often chosen on the basis of networks known and visible to those initiating them. And this can create its own democratic deficit. There is significant evidence (Brownill and Darke, 1998; Fitzpatrick et al, 1998; Henderson and Mayo, 1998) that certain groups are less well represented in partnership structures – particularly women, young people and people from an ethnic minority background. Professionals and policy makers may have made assumptions about how such groups can best be represented and about whether they can contribute to the 'strategic debate', without understanding the nature of these groups. Similarly, policy makers can fall into the tokenism trap of appointing one person or organisation to represent all minority groups or all women. Instead, effective partnership working needs to recognise the fact that race and gender are strategic regeneration issues. This is true for issues of representation. As Brownill and Darke observed:

Areas undergoing regeneration are likely to show more diversity than most locations with respect to ethnic mix and family type, as households subject to discrimination and disadvantage are forced into areas with problems which are avoided by those who can choose. Just as the experience of social economic and political exclusion is likely to be different for men and women are for different minority groups, so routes to inclusion and regeneration will differ. (1998)

Having adequate representation on the partnership board is an important first step to developing such an inclusive vision.

Business partners have little patience with 'talking shops', and can find the processes of consultation and decision making tedious and non-productive. Many are not interested in discussing the operational or detailed expenditure aspects of regeneration programmes, preferring to give their time to strategic development issues. The partnership leadership – particularly at a political level – can play a useful role in developing the links with individuals in the private sector. Effective, sustained business involvement often occurs when business representatives are organised before entering the partnership, for example through the local Chamber of Commerce or local business club (Carley et al, 2000). In some cases, however, the most successful private sector contribution comes from a committed individual, who will take on the role of 'link' with other businesses.

Institutional partners, such as public agencies and local authority strategic departments, have become 'partnership oriented' – sometimes to the point of partnership fatigue. But the local authority departmental 'silo' culture makes it difficult for strategic planners to commit some of their colleagues – for example, from education or social work. Health boards and trusts are beginning to participate, while, in most cases, other public services like the police, the Employment Service and the Benefits Agency need to be brought in. The government envisages that Local Strategic Partnerships will help ensure this type of coordination. It is crucial that mainstream service providers are brought into the partnership from the beginning – they will have responsibilities to provide services long after the regeneration partnership is over.

Agreeing structures and working style

The type of structures that are established, and the way in which they are determined, set the style of working for the partnership. The decision about the partnership structure, and the level of its formality (such as whether to create a separate company) often lies with those who take the lead. However, this should be an early decision for all of the partners, and should include how it is to be supported. Carley et al argue that:

> although seconded staff can make a valuable contribution, full-time paid staff able to operate with a degree of independence from any partner are better to promote the partnership's strategic programme and to make effective use of its human and financial resources. (2000)

The ARP studies show that partnership structures and working style can exclude as well as include. The under-representation, in most partnership structures, of women and ethnic minorities from the resident community is exacerbated by the over representation of white males from the other partners. The formal structures and how professionals operate these structures can be intimidating. Brownill and Darke (1998, p 16) include the following quote from a woman community representative from a previous study by R. Gilroy (1996) that demonstrates the dynamic between style and structure:

> "When I go [to board meetings] there is something about men in suits which makes me fall silent. I feel I can't speak because who will back me up, will they [the men in suits] agree or just put me down?" (1996, pp 248-58)

Partners within partnerships are not equal. Each partner brings, not only different experiences of formal meetings to the board table, but also a level of power. Supporting the community representatives should be a key concern of the partnership leadership. All the other partners round the table are likely to enjoy back-up bureaucracy, and a number of the ARP studies have called for some independent administrative support for the community representatives (see for example, Duncan and Thomas, 2000).

The different styles used by individual partners and their differing power bases are also likely to lead to conflicts within the partnership. In creating structures, the partnership must build in conflict resolution processes from the beginning.

Most partnerships have a formal board, but it should create a variety of mechanisms for collecting views and for broadening the decision-making processes. In addition to the more traditional newsletters, exhibitions and public meetings these may include:

- issue-based working groups;
- residents' surveys;
- Planning for Real®;
- focus groups;
- area and youth forums;
- citizens' juries.

Some of these – for example the area forums – may form the basis of long-term structures to improve local democracy which will survive the immediate partnership. They may become part of new neighbourhood management arrangements. And, by looking at wider democratic processes, it should be possible to keep the main partnership board to a manageable size of around 15 persons (Carley et al, 2000).

Finally, structures need to be regularly reviewed, used to share the leadership role, and manage key aspects of the regeneration strategy. However, structures are also affected by personalities. New members and the growing confidence of others can change the balance of power and partnerships need to be alive and sensitive to these changes.

Developing the relationships

Effective partnerships invest a considerable amount of energy and resources in developing trust and confidence between the partners. This may be regarded as 'training' or 'team-building'. It is not sufficient to undertake this only at the beginning of the partnership, but it should happen throughout the life of the partnership – particularly as board representatives change. Nor is training just for the board. One of the most effective styles is when a partnership board becomes a 'learning community', and that includes learning from each other. Too often professionals believe that 'capacity building' is an issue for local residents. Henderson and Mayo comment that:

Training is not necessarily identified as a key issue or built into regeneration strategies from the outset, let alone at the initial planning stage ... training plans have not necessarily started by identifying and building upon people's knowledge and skills. This is, potentially, a very dangerous omission – to imply that local people are 'empty vessels' simply waiting to be filled via training/capacity building ignores the wealth of existing knowledge and skills within communities. Nor has training been seen as a continuing process. (1998, p v)

Many professionals need to be trained in working with residents in deprived areas.

The most important part of team-building/training is the 'getting to know you' phase – understanding the other partners' motivation, culture and decision-making processes. Time spent on this creates a basis for trust and mutual confidence, and allows a culture that is unique to the partnership to be developed. It also enables the development of a 'vision' for the area – the first round of the shared agenda. Developing a vision (and translating it into workable objectives) is the real test of whether the relationships are going to lead to genuine partnership. It also recognises that different partners may have different priorities – particularly neighbourhood players who may have a very different view from the 'top-down' view of public agencies. Working in this way, the partnership has to be clear about the time-scales for the vision. Is it a vision time-limited by regeneration funding, or (preferably) a longer-term vision for the area which might include more durable neighbourhood management bodies, or perhaps new governance arrangements, all endorsed by the Local Strategic Partnership.

Vision building requires an understanding of the starting point. Challenge funding processes can force the pace at this stage, indeed can pre-empt a proper neighbourhood-led assessment. Carley et al considered that too few partnerships had developed the vision "in a systematic manner to produce consensual, workable medium, and short-term objectives, backed by commitments to finance, human resources, targets of achievement and monitoring systems" (2000). It is not sufficient for the strategy simply to list what is being done separately by the partners – the result of the partnership must be that the relationships

generate added value which comes from coordinated action or resource expenditure.

Staying committed

Effective partnerships depend on the commitment of the partners. This involves, not only the personal commitment of those who are 'delegated' to attend partnership boards, but the commitment of their organisation.

Organisational commitment is demonstrated by:

- Selecting representatives on the basis of inter-personal skills, including ensuring that he or she has a broad understanding of his or her own organisation
- Ensuring continuity of the partner's representative
- Being sensitive to issues of parity of levels between board members
- Ensuring that the partner's representative has delegated authority.

Keeping all the partners committed through the life of the regeneration programme will require a regular review of the roles that each plays. In particular, as confidence increases, the type of community participation may change. Similarly, the individual partner's views on strategic objectives may change and these may have to be revised. Continuous learning is a feature of successful partnerships. Carley et al describe it as

... not only about success and failure in regeneration strategy, by monitoring, but equally about the underlying values, reflected in working practices that partners bring to the table. (2000, p 22)

Commitment costs both time and financial resources. There is general recognition that resources are needed to ensure that key local players are involved, and to support the wide range of decision-making processes. Carley et al also found that effective regeneration requires an integrated approach to funding. The current public sector financial system, whereby local projects have to meet different national financial criteria for different agencies, does not encourage the kind of flexibility that partnership working requires. Carley argues that the time may be right for partners in a neighbourhood programme to work together towards a more innovative approach to funding the partnership. Could Local Strategic Partnerships contract with successful local partnerships to deliver block regeneration grants to them, thus allowing continuity, flexibility and innovation with the partnership effectively in charge? In this way commitment would matter.

Knowing how to part

The ARP studies did not spend time looking at how regeneration partnerships manage their ending. Most were concerned with getting started, while Carley et al (2000) investigated effectiveness during their operational life. But many partnerships are established for a short or fixed period of time, albeit seven to ten years. The end of the partnership will not be the end of the relationship between the agencies – particularly the local authority – and the local community. The regeneration programme may finish but life in the area goes on.

The measure of success of a regeneration partnership is whether the regeneration of the area has become sustainable. Planning for the ending of a partnership – the exit or forward strategy – is something that should be started long before the end date looms into view. Geoff Fordham, in an earlier study for the Foundation (Fordham, 1995), emphasises that:

- The chance of short-life regeneration programmes succeeding depends in part on an effective 'exit strategy' being planned and built into all activities.
- Long-term community involvement is essential to long-term sustainability.
- The crucial indicator of success may have nothing to do with physical regeneration, but may be the level of confidence, experience and skill that has been developed by the residents.
- Exits should be thought about as the regeneration process develops, and every individual project should incorporate an exit strategy into its development.
- There needs to be a focus within the area for continual regeneration. This may best be a community organisation, such as a Community Development Trust, into which the partnership could evolve over its life, or new neighbourhood management processes that will continue to exist and which will be the point for longer-term consultation. These can also monitor continuous improvement.

Realising the potential

Partnerships are a very human organisational model. They vary in style, quality and effectiveness. The ARP studies show that perfection is difficult to achieve; indeed there is no perfect model. The partnership will change, adapt and – hopefully – mature over time. Realising the potential of partnerships to deliver sustainable regeneration requires treating partnerships as relationships.

In adopting a partnership approach to regeneration, there are a number of recommendations that emerge from the ARP studies. To realise the potential requires government, partner organisations and partnership leaders to change the way they approach the use of partnerships:

- In assessing bids for regeneration programmes, and in monitoring the work of partnerships, government should give more emphasis to process. Bid assessment should include how the applicant leader intends to develop the relationships within the partnership. Monitoring should reflect local needs and processes, and not just central or local government requirements in respect of regeneration outputs or outcomes.

- Limiting the amount of bureaucracy involved with the bidding process, reporting and monitoring arrangements. Partnerships have to deal with different levels of government – local, central and European. They have to deal with Regional Development Agencies and regional Government Offices. Some partnerships have found ways to streamline the bureaucracy – new partnerships would benefit from guidance and support in this area.

- More recognition should be given to the time required for the relationships to develop, and the impact that these relationships might have on the vision and the objectives. Vision building should start with neighbourhood-led assessments.

- More recognition should be given to the inequalities of power within partnerships and to how the inevitable conflicts can be resolved.

- Race, gender and youth inclusion should be regarded as strategic partnership issues. Those assessing partnerships should develop equal opportunity 'badging' to ensure that partnerships are operating inclusively.

- Funding should be available at the beginning of the partnership for training and capacity building for both the community and other partners. The pace of funding should reflect local conditions. The possibility of block allocations of public funding to neighbourhood partnerships should be considered further. This might be considered in the context of Local Strategic Partnerships where more emphasis could be given to the linkages between neighbourhood partnerships and city- and region-wide strategies, and how the neighbourhood partnership can influence those strategies.

- Recognise that strategic objectives should be changeable to reflect community views, and that the role of the community should be reviewed as community confidence increases.

- Short-term regeneration partnerships should plan an 'exit' or 'forward' strategy.

5

The strategic dimension of area regeneration

Michael Carley

Summary

- There is real progress in regeneration, but the task is hampered by failure to integrate initiatives at national, regional, city-wide and neighbourhood levels.

- Physical regeneration that does not tackle the impact of manufacturing decline and the massive loss of full-time, manual jobs in industrial cities and towns is a problem. The benefits of economic growth are largely unavailable to these households, whose low incomes are a significant factor in social exclusion.

- Unfortunately, neither the Urban Task Force, the National Strategy for Neighbourhood Renewal (SEU, 1998), New Deal for Communities, nor recent HM Treasury statements suggest any sophisticated approach to this. It remains for the Urban White Paper team to undertake analysis which recognises development of the urban economic base, and investment in infrastructure, as key drivers of regeneration, even at the neighbourhood level.

- Many valuable regeneration partnerships have sprung up in the 1990s, but it should not be assumed that partnerships on their own can resolve urban problems. 'Partnership fatigue' is becoming common, in part from a failure to 'join up' initiatives nationally, reflected locally.

- Given progress in regional and city-level initiatives, an important task is to empower local neighbourhoods to play a valid, continuing role in neighbourhood management. Local government modernisation is essential to allow neighbourhoods to oversee services, while redefining the role of the local authority in a wholly constructive manner.

Policy implications

- The national policy framework requires continuing innovation towards a more strategic approach which grapples with urban renewal as a national objective; integrates policy streams and encourages flexible use of mainstream budgets; allocates resources to the investment in infrastructure from schools to public transport; and which, most importantly, devolves real control from the centre to the regional, city and local levels.

- For England, a timetable for statutory elected chambers may be necessary in order to give greater legitimacy to regional governance. Scotland and Wales need to develop more sophisticated mechanisms for linking local authorities and partners in a common effort in logical development regions.

- New Commitment to Regeneration has fostered some good practice in inter-local authority regeneration partnerships, but such initiatives need to be developed and supported financially in other travel-to-work sub-regions as appropriate, with particular emphasis on employment creation.

- The National Strategy for Neighbourhood Renewal, Community Planning and the Neighbourhood Renewal Fund all emphasise involving local communities in planning, implementation and management of local regeneration. But this will not happen unless the process is enabled by coordinated action at national, regional and local levels; new inclusive (and experimental) forms of neighbourhood management; and adequate resources for community development.

Two steps forward and *not* one step back?

An early study in the Area Regeneration Programme (ARP) noted with dismay that the current historical phase of formal urban regeneration policy in Britain was about to enter a fourth decade. This phase, of mainly area-based regeneration, could be said to have begun with the Housing Action Areas designated under the 1969 Housing Act. Given this long history, searching questions need to be asked about the effectiveness of the nation's approach to regeneration and why there are still far too many households and communities suffering from social exclusion (Carley and Kirk, 1998).

Recent developments suggest cause for optimism of real progress in the agenda of social inclusion. In the main, this is because the policy framework is finally recognising that area regeneration programmes may be necessary, but will never be sufficient, for area regeneration. Good bottom-up initiatives in communities – important in themselves – are seldom enough to achieve lasting regeneration in neighbourhoods and cities hard-hit by the decline of manufacturing and other dominant industries. Bottom-up and top-down must be linked in new and effective ways if social inclusion is to be achieved, and innovation must be pursued at all spatial levels of action from the national to the local.

As this chapter documents, a framework for pursuing innovation is emerging. An important regional structure has been initiated with the advent of Government Offices for the Regions, Regional Development Agencies and regional chambers and forums. In Scotland and Wales, devolution has created the opportunity for locally-tailored innovation. The "regional genie is out of the bottle" (Robson et al, 2000).

At the city-wide level, the Social Exclusion Unit (SEU) is proposing Local Strategic Partnerships which integrate community planning and regeneration and work at city-wide and local levels. In some cases, depending on the urban geography, 'city-wide' means partnerships of multiple local authorities including the county level. To be effective, the integration of community planning with regeneration will require attention to continued modernisation of local government – particularly the empowerment of local communities.

At the vital local level, the most progressive local authorities and their partners are refashioning the mechanisms of local democracy to allow effective and streamlined local participation in which local people have a real say in neighbourhood management and the quality of service delivery. This is a particularly exciting area because it holds out real possibility of creating a win-win situation which fosters both social inclusion and better local democratic processes. Local Strategic Partnerships (LSPs) need to be encouraged and supported in experimentation, for there are no right answers, only signposts and frameworks to help people work towards solutions in their own localities.

Perhaps the most important of these enabling frameworks is the national policy framework. It is here, perhaps, that the greatest degree of innovation is required – in the forthcoming Urban White Paper. It will be no help to move slightly and incrementally forward from the previous 30 years of policy. A more strategic approach is required which:

- grapples with urban decline and renewal as a national objective;
- integrates policy streams nationally and encourages flexible use of mainstream budgets;
- allocates sufficient resources to invest in infrastructure from schools to public transport;
- devolves real control from the centre to the regional, city and local levels.

Just as neighbourhoods need to be empowered by local authorities and their institutional partners, so Britain's cities and towns need to be empowered to get on with the job of developing innovative, locally appropriate methods of social inclusion and regeneration. Innovation and devolution go hand in hand in the modern world.

Integration – challenge at the heart of regeneration

The strategic aspects of regeneration have received close attention in the ARP. A key theme is the need for **enhanced integration**. This is required between:

- economic and physical development better linked to the agenda of social inclusion;
- long-term vision and strategy and the day-to-day activities of regeneration organisations;

- national, regional, city-wide and neighbourhood regeneration strategies and the activities of agencies and partnerships which promote these;
- local government, central agencies, the community and voluntary sector and the business community working in partnership;
- local government modernisation, that is, the mainstream activities of governance and democratic participation, including at the neighbourhood level, and regeneration initiatives and funding programmes.

This chapter explores these various aspects, concluding that enhanced integration will be secured from more effective linkage of policy and action at all spatial levels from the national to the neighbourhood. Perhaps the most important message is that there are no easy, off-the-peg answers to the difficult challenges of urban development and social inclusion. Solutions need to be as sophisticated as the problems are complex. One of the most fundamental aspects of this agenda is to redress the decline of employment opportunity in Britain's industrial city-regions.

Employment opportunity and urban decline

Low household income is a significant factor in social exclusion. If we ask how previously viable inner-city neighbourhoods and then-new council estates, to which people moved with enthusiasm in earlier decades, could have declined to the point of decrepitude and despair for many residents, the rise of unemployment is an important part of the answer. Across Britain, from East London's docks to the shipyards and steelworks of Strathclyde, the decline of traditional industry in urban areas is a marker of the growing need for physical, social and economic regeneration.

Important ARP studies have looked at employment trends and the decline of manufacturing. One study concluded that the long-standing labour market disparities between urban areas and the rest of Britain have widened steadily since the 1970s (Turok and Edge, 1999). Its most striking conclusion is that both relative and absolute declines in employment opportunity have not diminished in the past two decades,

despite expectations to the contrary. The inner areas of large conurbations are the worst hit, with steep declines in employment and a large-scale loss of full-time, male manual jobs.

Unemployment rates tell only half the story – non-employment in inner-city and industrial areas relative to the rest of the country is greater than suggested by unemployment figures alone (Green and Owen, 1998). There is also a racial dimension, given that more than half of African-Caribbean and Africans, and over a third of South Asians live in mixed tenure, inner-city districts with the highest rates of unemployment (Chahal, 2000).

The process of deindustrialisation has been supplemented by three related processes, all of which make inner-city regeneration more difficult:

- a decentralisation of economic activity as shops, offices and new, single-floor factories moved to suburban and greenfield locations;
- a shift of population from urban areas to suburban locations, market towns and rural areas;
- a concentration of the most socially deprived households in the worst estates and urban neighbourhoods, as prosperous households moved on.

The priority of need for regeneration is located squarely in the decline in manual employment which, research argues, is:

> ... the most important single issue facing urban Britain. Professional and managerial jobs have expanded, but are generally inaccessible to people who have experienced a loss of manual employment. (Turok and Edge, 1999, p 50)

There is little optimism that the urban policy framework recognises the true nature of the problem, with researchers pointing out that central government continues to perceive the difficulties of urban areas as 'essentially social' and confined to specific neighbourhoods. Other studies buttress this concern for an urban–regional perspective, stressing that land-use planning and inward investment policies, and investment in education and transport infrastructure, must be an essential aspect of any strategic plan to revitalise socially excluded areas of Britain's deindustrialised cities (Carley et al, 2000).

A main argument is that there is insufficient awareness of the economics of urban decline and spatial disparity between major, formerly industrial cities, and the rest of the country. Unfortunately, neither the report of the recent Urban Task Force (DETR, 1999), the National Strategy for Neighbourhood Renewal (NSNR) (SEU, 1998), the New Deal for Communities initiative, nor recent HM Treasury statements suggest any sophisticated approach to this dimension of the urban problem. It therefore remains for the Urban White Paper team to undertake the necessary integrated analysis which recognises development of the urban economic base and investment in infrastructure, as among the key drivers of regeneration – even at the neighbourhood level.

The record of urban policy

In addition to a concern about regeneration strategy, we noted that the ARP has been underpinned by an historical perspective. A number of studies began by asking how much was really being achieved by regeneration initiatives, locally and at an aggregate national level. One study charted a long list of urban policy initiatives going back to the 1960s and concluded that, although there were real achievements in physical regeneration, too little was being accomplished to reduce overall social exclusion (Carley et al, 2000). The NSNR has come to a similar conclusion, taking a neighbourhood perspective.

Another study noted "the limited success of area regeneration policies" and pointed to the *fragmented nature of governance* nationally and locally as a key problem (Hall and Mawson, 1999). Although there is much talk of 'joined-up' policy and practice, this fragmentation is a long way from being overcome at the beginning of the 21st century (Duncan and Thomas, 2000). The identified characteristics of the problem are striking:

- A proliferation of separate government initiatives and challenge funding regimes, described as bewildering at a local level, each with differing ministerial rules, regulations and participation mechanisms, imposing hidden human and financial costs on local regeneration.
- Departmentalism within local authorities and agencies resulting in poor local coordination.

- Failure to bend mainstream public expenditure to socially excluded areas.
- Failure to develop the necessary, multi-faceted regeneration strategies.
- Lack of a strategic city-region perspective to underpin area initiatives.

In addition to obvious measures of social exclusion, other implications are identified. There has been a steady withdrawal of private sector functions from deprived neighbourhoods with their replacements, such as credit unions or food cooperatives, not offering the same degree of choice which socially advantaged households take for granted (Speak and Graham, 2000).

There are growing areas of low demand for housing, a situation especially severe in the North of England (Niner, 1999). This is giving rise to what is termed 'area abandonment', where virtually nil demand for housing is generating a vicious cycle of falling school roles, loss of confidence and stigmatisation of areas, a vacuum in social control, anti-social behaviour and intense fear of crime (Power and Mumford, 1999). Even good quality, new or modernised houses are now being demolished in these blighted neighbourhoods. To turn this situation around will require a more integrated framework at regional, sub-regional and local levels, which links housing and labour market support programmes with forward-looking land-use and transport planning.

Joined-up policy or partnership fatigue?

In terms of governmental responses, ARP studies charted a continuing lack of policy coherence and coordination at the heart of a weak record of achievement. It is noted that, although there is pressure from central government for joined-up, *local* partnership working, there is little evidence of a joined-up *national* urban policy framework. Many ARP reports described 'an architecture of urban policy which is increasingly confused', 'partnership proliferation' stemming from 'a series of separately devised government initiatives', and recorded failures of integration between the DETR (then the Department of the Environment) and the Department of Trade and Industry going back 10 years or more (Parkinson, 1998; Hall and Mawson, 1999; Carley et al, 2000).

The intention to achieve national policy objectives through local partnerships is being undermined by what is described as 'partnership fatigue' at both neighbourhood and city level. Some local authorities describe having over 100 partnerships on the go simultaneously. These bring benefits, but at a large cost of the human resources needed to form and implement partnerships. Partnership proliferation is confusing for local residents who would prefer a simple participation framework which delivers the goods on a systematic basis.

Top-down support – the regional framework

One dilemma for regeneration is how to integrate area-based programmes, favoured in urban policy, with wider conurbation and regional level strategies which are essential to restore economic vitality and to link economic, social and physical development to best advantage (Parkinson, 1998; Carley and Kirk, 1998). Another dilemma is how to target economic development efforts on the localities with the highest unemployment, not simply the greenfield sites where the private property development industry is keenest to invest (Turok and Edge, 1999).

The ARP provided some of the first constructive reviews of the emerging regional development framework in England. Despite the establishment of Regional Development Agencies (RDAs) in 1999, the framework remains weak and confused (Carley et al, 2000; Robson et al, 2000). One problem is that there is not enough clarity over the respective roles of different agencies:

- Government Offices for the Regions (GORs), which oversee Regional Planning Guidance and transport strategy, as well as joined-up policy between central departments.
- The new RDAs which produce regional economic strategies, which, research suggests, are as yet insufficiently robust statements, and whose budgets are mainly drawn from resources targeted at regeneration, rather than economic development *per se*.
- Regional chambers and forums, some of the former pre-dating but now attached to RDAs, which may one day be statutory elected chambers. Some chambers already have staff which engage in regional development activities and forward planning.

Lack of clear organisational responsibility means lack of agreement on which should be the lead agency in the regional sustainable development planning which needs to underpin city and area regeneration. This planning process includes not only influence over inward investment and the balance between greenfield and brownfield development, but ensuring that transport and land-use planning, for example over the location of new retail facilities, serves both social inclusion and quality of life agendas.

There is a reasonable argument in having GORs, work closely with chambers, as lead agencies in the regions, ensuring a pattern of sustainable development which enhances quality of life for all residents and the attractiveness of the city-region to inward investors, but also addresses issues of local governance as they affect area regeneration. The RDAs could then focus on more specific issues of economic development linked to training, education and lifelong learning, at regional, city and neighbourhood levels. The necessary definition of roles, and link between concentrated area regeneration and urban development as a whole, remains unclear.

Two ARP studies identified a pivotal, and largely unacknowledged, role for GORs in providing links between central departments and regeneration partnerships (Carley and Kirk, 1998; Hall and Mawson, 1999). However, links between GORs and community initiatives needed to be stronger, and the recent announcement giving GORs a stronger role in coordinating the NSNR is a step in this direction. It remains to be seen whether GORs will have the sanctioning powers necessary to persuade centralist local authorities to pursue decentralised, community-based approaches. Many currently lack staff with community development expertise or experience of working at the community level (Duncan and Thomas, 2000). Both points need to be rectified if the neighbourhood approach of the NSNR is to be achieved.

RDAs appear to be securing increasing control over regeneration funding, such as Single Regeneration Budget (SRB). However, there is said to be little evidence that they understand how to handle relationships with local regeneration partnerships (Robson et al, 2000). Many *local voices* in regeneration, from the voluntary sector, community groups and even within regeneration partnerships, are said to feel that they exert little or no influence on RDAs and, therefore, are being excluded from developing regeneration strategy and partnership at this important level.

An ambiguity is identified in the mission of RDAs, which may influence their ability to achieve regional regeneration (Robson et al, 2000). On the one hand, their role could be to address the core issue of regional disparity, for example, between booming London and northern city-regions. But each RDA has been given an equal mandate which is the same across England – in prosperous as well as deprived regions, with no additional powers or resources in the latter. On the other hand, the establishment of a common, country-wide framework suggests that RDAs are actually part of a devolutionary process – in parallel with the political devolution of Scotland, Wales and Northern Ireland. This devolutionary intent is said to be "more token than real" (Robson et al, 2000), as the government shies away from further devolution to the English regions. One impact of a tokenistic approach is the failure to resolve organisational roles. For regeneration, confusion about role limits the ability to provide the coherent development framework identified by many studies as necessary to support local regeneration.

Turning to Scotland and Wales, a study compared regeneration in these countries with that in England (Carley et al, 2000). The report argues that, while Scotland and Wales gained nationally in terms of new Parliaments giving opportunity for more joined-up policy, they lost in the recent local government reorganisation which swept away regional government, such as in Strathclyde or the South Wales Valleys, in favour of small, unitary authorities (nine in the former Strathclyde and nine in the Valleys). The effect is that regions with many local authorities and neighbourhoods suffering social exclusion are disadvantaged by lack of regional strategic planning. For example, employment opportunities created by inward investment in one local authority – often seeing itself in competition with its neighbours – frequently can be inaccessible by affordable public transport from neighbouring areas of high unemployment, because no agency is empowered to integrate the two.

Partnership at the city-wide level

Just as deindustrialised cities need the support of regional economic development, serious local problems, such as area abandonment, need an over-arching structure "for managing conditions and orchestrating change" (Power and Mumford, 1999). City-wide regeneration strategies, including social housing allocation policies, are required to avoid merely displacing social problems from one area to another. They are also important in the attraction of private finance into regeneration, where a major concern is that investment in one area risks being degraded by lack of regeneration in a neighbouring area (Adair and Berry, 1998).

City-wide partnerships, at their best, have been found to provide a valuable strategic framework for area regeneration, promoting leadership, vision and the development of consensus around key issues, in and between neighbouring local authorities, bringing stakeholders into partnership and providing coherence in service delivery at the local authority level (Carley and Kirk, 1998). City Pride initiatives in Birmingham and Manchester have been cited for encouraging city-wide partnership, in the latter between four local authorities. However, a comparison of Britain with Europe suggests that city-wide partnerships ought to have more formal status, with national commitment to partnership substantial and long term (Parkinson, 1998).

The cross-cutting LSP proposed in the NSNR could provide the framework for taking forward partnership at various levels, including the city-wide level. The SEU's suggestion that these LSPs be responsible for community planning is a good one, providing there is coherence across programmes and the number of partnerships needed is simplified.

Bringing community into local governance

In the strategic regeneration framework, it is action at the neighbourhood level which is the frontline in the fight for social inclusion. Residents of the poorest estates are found to suffer disproportionately high levels of disadvantage, with complex needs which require substantial agency coordination and collaborative service planning (Gregory, 1998). Agencies working at all levels need to be aware of the implications of their work for deprived neighbourhoods, and to encourage participation. For example, a review of Urban Development Corporations found that the Tyne and Wear Development Corporation programme had a strong community strategy, built on early consultation and joint working, which "permeated all aspects of its work" (Russell, 1998). This led to a more equitable and effective development programme with greater local ownership than in other Urban Development Corporations.

A summary in the ARP Foundations series identified the importance of transforming mainstream services at the local level via local partnerships, and of policy integration at the neighbourhood level (Taylor, 2000). Research teams have identified two levels of integration:

- *At the neighbourhood level:* **neighbourhood management**, giving rise to local service agreements which formally link community, local government and other institutional stakeholders.
- *At the local authority level:* formal and informal processes of **local government modernisation**, essential to allow neighbourhoods to be empowered to engage in self-management.

Neighbourhood management

Neighbourhood management is identified as one of the 'big ideas' in the government's campaign to tackle social exclusion and a key plank of the NSNR. The building blocks of this process identified by the ARP are:

- new governance structures at the local level;
- joined-up systems for implementation;
- flexible working practices;
- sufficient resources;
- a supportive institutional infrastructure at city, regional and national levels (Taylor, 2000).

Within this context, local service agreements or Community Plans ought to connect local residents to all the local agencies of service delivery (Hall and Mawson, 1999). Substantial consultation with residents will lead to a redefinition of the goals for the neighbourhood and of problems faced locally, and formal agreements with service providers in terms of expenditure, standards and monitoring of

achievement, with periodic reviews. An element of community development may be necessary initially, but the service agreement can become a long-term, permanent linkage between community and service agencies. However, community participation in many current regeneration programmes is said to be 'chaotic' and research calls for "a one-stop participation process" to establish priorities for local development and to allow residents to be involved in neighbourhood management on a lifelong basis, if they so wish (Carley and Kirk, 1998).

Demonstration projects of local service agreements in Burnley and area coordination in Coventry showed that these were an effective means of addressing pressing concerns of residents on disadvantaged estates (Gregory, 1998). They increased residents' influence as service users, but also strengthened local democracy by restoring faith in these local authority led projects.

A related innovation is the proposal for Social Enterprise Zones (SEZs), now in pilot status in the London Borough of Newham (Robinson et al, 1998). This project addresses the potential contribution of mainstream government budgets to regeneration. Under current arrangements, resources such as benefits and housing budgets represent enormous expenditure, but, rather than being ladders out of poverty, keep people locked into patterns of deprivation. SEZs involve local residents in review and management of mainstream services, not just from the local authority, but from central agencies such the Benefits Agency, which are given a mandate from HM Treasury and the Audit Commission to act in a flexible manner and vire monies between budgets and years. "Integrated spending patterns" are to be evaluated as well as those of individual agencies.

Local government modernisation

The NSNR identifies problems in deprived neighbourhoods as deriving, in part, from the failure of core services and the lack of clear strategy and concerted joint action. These issues will be tackled by LSPs. ARP research supports this, arguing that, although a minority of areas might achieve regeneration without local government involvement, to tackle social exclusion systematically requires local government modernisation to be seen as a 'foundation stone' of regeneration (Carley et al, 2000). A four-fold modernisation agenda is involved.

Modernisation agenda

- Good leadership in establishing a long-term vision for the local authority and its neighbourhoods, with full and open participation, translating this into a practical Community Plan, or development strategy.

- Formulating the local authority's responsibilities into a detailed corporate strategy, which links together single departments in a coordinated agenda, with targets for assessing achievement, which is then disaggregated to a neighbourhood level.

- Rethinking the processes of local democracy and the roles of local councillors, especially those outside the new cabinets, so they feel able to work closely with local community organisations.

- Devolving service delivery to partner organisations, and/or to local communities, with a measure of budgeting control and within the framework of Best Value and neighbourhood management.

Although explicitly recognising the problems of deprived neighbourhoods, the NSNR may be in danger of implying that neighbourhood management in deprived areas, although necessary, will be sufficient in itself to achieve regeneration. ARP research suggests that equal attention to the working of local authorities and joined-up government in town halls are the necessary foundations for neighbourhood management, and that improvements in local democracy need to extend across all neighbourhoods to have political credibility.

Key recommendations

This chapter noted that a key requirement in fostering strategic regeneration is integration, and mentioned five types of integration, discussed throughout the chapter. Enhanced integration will stem in part from strong leadership at all levels, beginning with strong leadership from central government. The NSNR is rather weak in this regard, contenting itself with mention of "oversight from Whitehall".

Whitehall needs to do more: to integrate its own programmes in a coherent manner, to question whether the way it formulates policy and funds regeneration is the most effective, to provide flexibility in use of mainstream budgets, to lead on the knowledge base of what works and what does not, to encourage transfer of good practice and to wield sanctions if necessary.

Area regeneration may never be sustainable outside a coordinated regional development framework. It is therefore appropriate to go forward in a bold, positive manner, to establish solid and sensible working relationships between GORs, RDAs, chambers and other regional bodies, rather than shying away from so doing because of difficulties of devolution. A timetable for statutory elected chambers may be necessary in order to give greater legitimacy to regional governance. It is also important to audit regeneration at the regional level and to support and encourage local good practice. Scotland and Wales need to develop more sophisticated mechanisms for linking local authorities and partners in a common effort in logical development regions such as the South Wales Valleys or Greater Glasgow urban region (Carley et al, 2000).

At the metropolitan region and city-wide level, more integrated approaches need to be encouraged by central government, GORs and RDAs. City Pride and New Commitment to Regeneration have fostered some good practice in inter-local authority regeneration partnerships, but such initiatives need to be developed and supported financially in other travel-to-work sub-regions as appropriate, with particular emphasis on employment creation. Additional research may be necessary to help us understand how to achieve economic development *and* social inclusion simultaneously, with public investment as a catalyst to market activity.

Local government modernisation is vitally important to support neighbourhood management – with democratic empowerment for neighbourhood management and with integrated, efficient service delivery. This needs to link local councillors and communities in a positive, forward-looking way. There is no one right way to do this – experimentation in local governance will be necessary, with a constructive, action-research component built into a wide variety of initiatives. The proposed LSPs could be a good means of achieving better local democracy and area regeneration, while reducing the need for every regeneration programme to have a separate community participation aspect. Local people want streamlined, highly effective participation – not a bewildering multiplicity of initiatives which sap local resources to little avail.

Effective community development for regeneration requires strengthening of the network of intermediary agencies involved in neighbourhood regeneration. RDAs are said to be in a position to play a key role here, to support the development of such agencies and to help transfer good practice from region to region and town to town (Duncan and Thomas, 2000).

The NSNR, the Community Planning initiative and the Neighbourhood Renewal Fund all place heavy emphasis on involving local communities in planning, implementation and management of local regeneration. But this will not happen unless the process is enabled by coordinated action at national, regional and local levels; new inclusive (and experimental) forms of neighbourhood management; and adequate resources for community development. Central government's role could include giving authorisation for centrally-controlled agencies, such as the Benefits Agency, to operate flexibly at the local level according to locally-defined needs.

This last point returns the chapter to its main theme of integration – stressing that the positive or negative impacts of regeneration policy and action at all levels are felt most keenly in the nation's deprived neighbourhoods. Continued progress in good governance, and partnership at every spatial level is therefore important. It is a collective national responsibility to ensure that this framework of policy and action tackles social exclusion in the most effective manner possible.

References

Adair, A. and Berry, J. (1998) *Accessing private finance: The availability and effectiveness of private finance in urban regeneration*, Coventry: RICS Books.

Anastacio, J., Gidley, B., Hart, L., Keith, M., Mayo, M. and Kowarzik, U. (2000) *Reflecting realities: Participants' perspectives on integrated communities and sustainable development*, Bristol/York: The Policy Press/JRF.

Andersen, H., Munck, R., Fagan, C., Goldson, B., Hall, D., Lansley, J., Novak, T., Melville, R., Moore, R. and Ben-Tovim, G. (1999) *Neighbourhood images in Liverpool: 'It's all down to the people'*, York: York Publishing Service/JRF.

Beatty, C. and Fothergill, S. (1999) *Labour market detachment among older men*, Sheffield: CRESR, Sheffield Hallam University.

Bennett, K., Beynon, H. and Hudson, R. (2000) *Coalfields regeneration: Dealing with the consequences of industrial decline*, Bristol/York: The Policy Press/JRF.

Brownill, S. and Darke, J. (1998) *'Rich mix': Inclusive strategies for urban regeneration*, Bristol/York: The Policy Press/JRF.

Burns, D. and Taylor, M. (2000) *Auditing community participation: An assessment handbook*, Bristol/York: The Policy Press/JRF.

Burrows, R. and Rhodes, D. (1998) *Unpopular places? Area disadvantage and the geography of misery in England*, Bristol/York: The Policy Press/JRF.

Campbell, M. (1999) *The third sector, jobs and local development*, Synthesis Report for DG Employment and Social Affairs, European Commission.

Campbell, M. (2000a) *Partnership for success: A good practice guide*, London: DfEE.

Campbell, M. (2000b) 'The third sector, jobs and local development: the European experience', Paper presented to International Society for Third Sector Research, Dublin, 4-8 July.

Campbell, M. (2000c) *Learning pays and learning works*, Sheffield: NACETT.

Campbell, M. and Meadows, P. (2000) *What works locally? The policy agenda*, York: York Publishing Service/JRF.

Campbell, M. and Sanderson, I. (2000) 'The jobs gap and structural unemployment', Appendix 19 in House of Commons Education and Employment Committee, *Fourth Report: Employability and jobs: Is there a jobs gap?*, London: The Stationery Office.

Campbell, M., Sanderson, I. and Walton, F. (1998) *Local responses to long term unemployment*, York: York Publishing Service/JRF.

Carley, M. and Kirk, K. (1998) *Sustainable by 2020?*, Bristol/York: The Policy Press/JRF.

Carley, M., Chapman, M., Hastings, A., Kirk, K. and Young, R. (2000) *Urban regeneration through partnership: A study in nine urban regions in England, Scotland and Wales*, Bristol/York: The Policy Press/JRF.

Cattell, V. and Evans, M. (1999) *Neighbourhood images in East London: Social capital and social networks on two East London estates*, York: York Publishing Service/JRF.

Chahal, K. (2000) *Ethnic diversity, neighbourhood and housing*, York: JRF.

Dean, J. and Hastings, A. (2000) *Challenging images: Housing estates, stigma and regeneration*, Bristol/York: The Policy Press/JRF.

DETR (Department of the Environment, Transport and the Regions) (1999) *Towards an urban renaissance: Final report of the Urban Task Force*, London: DETR.

DETR (2000) *Our towns and cities: The future: delivering an urban renaissance*, London: DETR.

DfEE (Department for Education and Employment) (2000a) *Jobs for all: Report for the Jobs Policy Action Team*, London: DfEE.

DfEE (2000b) *Action teams for jobs*, London: DfEE.

Duncan, P. and Thomas, S. (2000) *Neighbourhood regeneration: Resourcing community involvement*, Bristol/York: The Policy Press/JRF.

Education and Employment Commission (2000) *Employability and jobs: Is there a jobs gap?*, London: The Stationery Office.

Fitzpatrick, S., Hastings, A., and Kintrea, K. (1998) *Including young people in urban regeneration: A lot to learn?*, Bristol/York: The Policy Press/JRF.

Fordham, G. (1995) *Made to last: Creating sustainable neighbourhoods and estate regeneration*, York: JRF.

Forrest, R. and Kearns, A. (1999) *Joined up places? Social cohesion and neighbourhood regeneration*, York: York Publishing Service/JRF.

Freire, P. (1970) *Pedagogy of the oppressed*, New York, NY: Herder and Herder.

Gilroy, R. (1996) 'Build routes to power', *Local Economy*, vol 11, no 3.

Green, A.E. and Owen, D. (1998) *Where are the jobless? Changing unemployment and non-employment in cities and regions*, Bristol/York: The Policy Press/JRF.

Gregg, P. and Wadsworth, J. (1998) 'Unemployment and non employment', *Employment Policy Institute Economic Report*, vol 12, no 6.

Gregory, S. (1998) *Transforming local services: Partnership in action*, York: York Publishing Services/JRF.

Hall, S. and Mawson, J. (1999) *Challenge funding, contracts and area regeneration: A decade of innovation in policy management and coordination*, Bristol/York: The Policy Press/JRF.

HCEEC (House of Commons Education and Employment Committee) (2000a) *Employability and jobs: Is there a jobs gap, Vol 1 Report and Proceedings*, London: House of Commons HC60-I.

HCEEC (2000b) *Employability and jobs: Is there a jobs gap, Vol 2: Minutes of evidence and appendices*, London: House of Commons HC60-II.

Henderson, P. and Mayo, M. (1998) *Training and education in urban regeneration: A framework for participants*, Bristol/York: The Policy Press/JRF.

HM Treasury (2000) *The goal of full employment: Employment opportunity for all*, London: HM Treasury.

Holmans, A. and Simpson, M. (1999) *Low demand – Separating fact for fiction*, Coventry/York: Chartered Institute of Housing/JRF.

Hutchinson, J. and Campbell, M. (1998) *Working in partnerships: Lessons from the literature*, DfEE Research Report RR63, London: DfEE.

JRF (Joseph Rowntree Foundation) (1995) *Inquiry into income and wealth, Volume 1*, York: JRF.

JRF (1998) *Regenerating neighbourhoods: Creating integrated and sustainable improvements*, Foundations 588, York: JRF.

JRF (1999) *Developing effective community involvement strategies: Guidance for Single Regeneration Budget bids*, Summary 169, York: JRF.

JRF (2000a) 'Resourcing community involvement in neighbourhood regeneration', Findings 320, York: JRF.

JRF (2000b) *Tackling social exclusion at local level: Neighbourhood management*, Summary 310, York: JRF.

Leadbetter, C. and Martin, S. (1998) *The employee mutual: Combining flexibility with security in the world of work*, London: Demos.

Lee, P. and Murie, A. (1997) *Poverty, housing tenure and social exclusion*, Bristol/York: The Policy Press/JRF.

Lee, P., Murie, A. and Gordon, D. (1995) *Area measures of deprivation: A study of current methods and best practices in the identification of poor areas in Great Britain*, Birmingham: Centre for Urban and Regional Studies, University of Birmingham.

Macfarlane, R. (1997) *Unshackling the poor: A complementary approach to local economic development*, York: York Pulishing Service/JRF.

Macfarlane, R. (2000a) *Local jobs from local development: The use of planning agreements to target training and employment outcomes*, York: York Publishing Service/JRF.

Macfarlane, R. (2000b) *Using local labour in construction: A good practice resource book*, Bristol/York: The Policy Press/Joseph Rowntree Foundation.

MacGillivray, A., Conaty, P. and Wadhams, L. (2000: forthcoming) *Low flying heroes*, London: New Economics Foundation.

Maclennan, D. (2000) *Changing places, engaging people*, York: York Publishing Service/JRF.

McGregor, A. and Maclennan, D. (1992) *Strategic approaches to urban regeneration*, Edinburgh: Scottish Homes.

McGregor, A., Glass, A, Richmond, K., Ferguson, Z. and Higgins, K. (1999) *Employer involvement in area regeneration*, Bristol/York: The Policy Press/JRF.

Niner, P. (1999) *Insights into lower demand for housing*, Foundations 739, York: JRF.

Oc,T., Tiesdell, S. and Moynihan, D. (1997) *Urban regeneration and ethnic minority groups: Training and business support in City Challenge areas*, Bristol/York: The Policy Press/JRF.

OECD (Organisation for Economic Co-operation and Development) (1998) *Local management for more effective employment policy*, Paris: OECD.

OECD (1999) *The local dimension of welfare to work*, Paris: OECD.

Parkinson, M. (1998) *Combating social exclusion: Lessons from area-based programmes in Europe*, Bristol/York: The Policy Press/JRF.

Phillips, S. (1992) *Tenants together: Tenant participation and council housing*, London: Department of the Environment.

Plummer, J. and Zipfel, T. (1998) *Regeneration and employment: A new agenda for TECs, communities and partnerships*, Bristol/York: The Policy Press/JRF.

Power, A. and Mumford, K. (1999) *The slow death of great cities? Urban abandonment or urban renaissance*, York: York Publishing Services/JRF.

Richardson, K. and Corbishley, P. (1999) *Frequent moving: Looking for love?*, York: York Publishing Service/JRF.

Robinson, D., Dunn, K. and Ballantyne, S. (1998) *Social enterprise zones: Building innovation into regeneration*, York: York Publishing Services/JRF.

Robson, B., Peck, J. and Holden, A. (2000) *Regional agencies and area-based regeneration*, Bristol/York: The Policy Press/JRF.

Russell, H. (1998) *A place for the community?: Tyne and Wear Development Corporation's approach to regeneration*, Bristol/York: The Policy Press/JRF.

Sanderson, I., Walton, F. and Campbell, M. (1999) *Back to work: Local action on unemployment*, York: York Publishing Service/JRF.

Saunders, R. (1997) *Resident services organisations: A new tool for regeneration*, Manchester: Priority Estates Project.

Scott, S., Clapham, D., Clark, A., Goodlad, R., Parkey, H., Rodgers, D. and Williams, M. (1994) *The guide to the right to manage*, London: HMSO.

SEU (Social Exclusion Unit) (1998) *Bringing Britain together: A national strategy for neighbourhood renewal*, Cm 4045, London: Cabinet Office.

SEU (2000a) *National strategy for neighbourhood renewal: Report of Policy Action Team 16: Learning lessons*, London: Cabinet Office.

SEU (2000b) *National strategy for neighbourhood renewal: A framework for consultation*, London: Cabinet Office.

SEU (2000c) *National Strategy for Neighbourhood Renewal: Report of Policy Action Team 4: neighbourhood management*, London: Cabinet Office.

SEU (2000d) *National Strategy for Neighbourhood Renewal: Report of the Policy Action Team on Jobs*, London: Cabinet Office.

Silburn, R., Lucas, D. Page, R. and Hanna, L. (1999) *Neighbourhood images in Nottingham: Social cohesion and neighbourhood change*, York: York Publishing Service/JRF.

Speak, S. and Graham, S. (2000) *Service not included: Social implications of private sector service restructuring in marginalised neighbourhoods*, Bristol/York: The Policy Press/JRF.

Taylor, M. (2000) *Top down meets bottom up: Neighbourhood management*, York: JRF.

Turok, I. and Edge, N. (1999) *The jobs gap in Britain's cities: Employment loss and labour market consequences*, Bristol/York: The Policy Press/JRF.

Ward, M. (1997) *A public policy framework for community based regeneration*, Housing Briefing Paper, September, York: JRF.

Wilkinson, R. (1994) *Unfair shares*, London: Barnardo's.

Williams, C.C. and Windebank, J. (1999) *A helping hand: Harnessing self-help to combat social exclusion*, York: York Publishing Service/JRF.

Wood, M. (1994) 'Should tenants take over? Radical community work, tenants organisations and the future of public housing', in S. Jacobs and K. Popple (eds) *Community work in the 1990s*, Nottingham: Spokesman.

Wood, M. (1996) 'Talking with tenants: options for public housing in the nineties', in *Talking Point*, no 164, January.

Wood, M. and Vamplew, C. (1999) *Neighbourhood images in Teesside: Regeneration or decline?*, York: York Publishing Service/JRF.

Appendix: Projects in the Area Regeneration Programme

Notes

- The Area Regeneration Programme ran between 1996 and 2001. It supported over 60 projects representing an investment of well over £2 million

- It has not been possible in this overview report to reference every report within the Programme, however, it was felt that the reader would welcome an annotated list of all ARP projects. Those reports referenced in *Regeneration in the 21st century* are in shaded boxes (those *not* are in outlined boxes)

- The Foundations and Findings documents which summarise most reports can be accessed on the Joseph Rowntree Foundation's website at www.jrf.org.uk

- All publications are published in association with the Joseph Rowntree Fiundation

Adair, Alasdair and Berry, James (1998) *Accessing private finance: The availability and effectiveness of private finance in urban regeneration*, RICS Books.

Findings 558: 'Attracting private finance into urban regeneration'

Private sector investment is an essential component in the effective delivery of urban regeneration and represents a central theme in current government policy. However, urban regeneration has traditionally been perceived as a high-risk, low-return investment. This study, by researchers at the Centre for Property Planning at the University of Ulster, examines the use of initiatives; influences on investment decision making; and perceptions of those involved in the regeneration process.

Anastacio, Jean; Gidley, Ben; Hart, Lorraine; Keith, Michael; Mayo, Marjorie and Kowarzik, Ute (2000) *Reflecting realities: Participants' perspectives on integrated communities and sustainable development*, The Policy Press.

Findings 770: 'Community participants' perspectives on involvement in area regeneration programmes'

This study explores the experiences of residents involved in urban regeneration projects and suggests that there is still much to learn about involving local people in regeneration initiatives. This project was carried out in parallel with another ARP project by Danny Burns and Marilyn Taylor entitled *Auditing community participation*.

Andersen, Helen; Munck, Ronnie et al (1999) *Neighbourhood images in Liverpool: "It's all down to the people"*, York Publishing Services.

Findings 479: 'Neighbourhood images in Liverpool'

There is a growing recognition that the needs, aspirations and potential of people and communities in disadvantaged areas need to be taken into account if urban regeneration is to become sustainable. This study of two neighbourhoods in Liverpool, conducted by researchers from the University of Liverpool, examines the residents' own perceptions in this regard. The work was carried out in parallel with three other research projects in Teesside, East London and Nottingham; all four projects were summarised in an overview report (Forrest and Kearns, 1999).

Bennett, Katy; Beynon, Hew and Hudson, Ray (2000) *Coalfields regeneration: Dealing with the consequences of industrial decline*, The Policy Press.

Findings 450: 'Coalfields regeneration: dealing with the consequences of industrial decline'

During the 1990s, coalmining employment collapsed dramatically. This removed at a stroke the economic rationale of coalfield places, ruptured their social fabric and precipitated a deep sense of loss. The researchers have evaluated the impacts of both regeneration policies and community initiatives in these areas.

Bevan, Mark and Gilroy, Rose (2000) *Industrial renaissance and community benefit: A story of the York Regeneration Partnership*, York Publishing Services.

Findings 040: 'Towards a regeneration strategy for York'

York Regeneration Partnership took root in a city without a long record of multi-agency regeneration projects and which showed some reluctance to identify deprivation as a city-wide problem. By the end of the partnership, partners had moved to a position where they were championing the need for a robust city-wide regeneration strategy. This study provides an honest account of how one SRB partnership developed over four years and pays particular attention to the role of the community within this partnership.

Brownill, Sue and Darke, Jane (1998) *'Rich mix': Inclusive strategies for urban regeneration*, The Policy Press.

Findings 0108: 'Inclusive strategies for race and gender in urban regeneration'

Issues of race and gender remain marginalised within regeneration policy, despite increasing emphasis on social inclusion. This study, based at Oxford Brookes University, reviewed existing research to discover how proper understanding of diversity can inform regeneration strategies.

Burns, Danny and Taylor, Marilyn (1998) *Mutual aid and self-help: Coping strategies for excluded communities*, The Policy Press.

Findings: 928: 'The role of mutual aid and self-help in combating exclusion'

Mutual aid and self-help are often seen as the answer to problems of economic and social exclusion. But can society find ways of encouraging them without changing their nature? A review by Danny Burns and Marilyn Taylor looks at what we already know about these informal activities and networks, and the implications for policy and practice.

Burns, Danny and Taylor, Marilyn (2000) *Auditing community participation: An assessment handbook*, The Policy Press.

This project accompanied the report by Jean Anastacio et al – *Reflecting realities* – referenced on page 54. In this project, Danny Burns and Marilyn Taylor developed a set of audit tools to test how far good practice in community participation is being followed in regeneration partnerships. There are plans to test run these audit tools in 2001 'for real' in an English region.

Burrows, Roger and Rhodes, David (1998) *Unpopular places? Area disadvantage and the geography of misery in England*, The Policy Press.

Findings 0118: 'Patterns of neighbourhood dissatisfaction in England'

What are the main sources of neighbourhood dissatisfaction in England? What sort of people are the most likely to be dissatisfied with their neighbourhoods? This research looks at patterns of neighbourhood dissatisfaction in England, using data from the Survey of English Housing in combination with data from the Census. The research was carried out by a team from the University of York.

Carley, Michael and Kirk, Karryn (1998) *Sustainable by 2020? A strategic approach to urban regeneration for Britain's cities*, The Policy Press.

Findings 638: 'Towards a long-term, strategic approach to urban regeneration'

Despite 30 years of short-term urban regeneration programmes, many areas are still characterised by deprivation. This research programme in city-wide regeneration, with case studies in Birmingham, Manchester, Glasgow and Edinburgh, aimed to identify which elements can make regeneration strategies more sustainable in the long term.

Carley, Michael; Chapman, Mike; Hastings, Annette; Kirk, Karryn and Young, Raymond (2000) *Urban regeneration through partnership: A study in nine urban regions in England, Scotland and Wales*, The Policy Press.

Foundations 560: 'Urban regeneration through partnership: a critical appraisal'

An enduring need for urban regeneration despite 30 years of regeneration activity, raises the question of whether we are organising ourselves sufficiently, as a society, to achieve successful regeneration over the next 30 years. Although there was an explosion in the 1990s in the use of partnerships as a means to regenerate, not enough is known about why some partnerships are effective and others are not. The conclusions reached by this study of 27 partnerships in nine city regions, identify key lessons for better partnership and critical issues about policy and governance which affect the future of Britain's cities.

Cattell, Vicky and Evans, Mel (1999) *Neighbourhood images in East London: Social capital and social networks on two East London estates*, York Publishing Services.

Findings 499: 'Neighbourhood images in East London'

A study of two estates in East London found a picture of vibrant and complex community life. The study focused on the views and experiences of local people, their perceptions of neighbourhood, social networks and involvement with the community. The research illustrates both variation and consensus within and between two neighbourhoods in regeneration areas and explores the underlying influences. This project was carried out in parallel with three other similar neighbourhood projects in Teesside, Liverpool and Nottingham; all four projects were summarised in an overview report (Forrest and Kearns, 1999).

Chahal, Kusminder (2000)

Foundations 110: 'Ethnic diversity, neighbourhoods and housing'

In this summary document, Kusminder Chahal brings together the main findings of recent Joseph Rowntree Foundation projects that examined the social and economic experiences of ethnic minority groups. Although many people will be aware of the issues raised, the persistence of some difficulties suggests that greater attention needs to be paid to them by mainstream services and more account taken of them in the formation of general economic social policy.

Dean, Jo and Hastings, Annette (2000) *Challenging images: Housing estates stigma and regeneration*, The Policy Press.

Findings 020: 'Challenging images: housing estates, stigma and regeneration'

Many of the UK's worst housing estates do not simply endure material disadvantage but also suffer from poor reputations. Viewed as 'problem places' home to 'problem people', such a reputation can reinforce an estate's difficulties. This report by a team at the University of Glasgow, examines three stigmatised estates undergoing regeneration programmes and explores how regenerations can address image problems.

Dorsett, Richard (1998) *Ethnic minorities in the inner city*, The Policy Press.

Findings 988: 'Ethnic minorities in the inner city'

Most of Britain's ethnic minority population now lives in the major cities, particularly inner cities. Given the high levels of deprivation in inner cities, most tend to live in deprived areas. This analysis explores where concentrations of people from different ethnic minority groups are likely to occur and examines the factors which influence this.

Duncan, Pete and Thomas, Sally (2000) *Neighbourhood regeneration: Resourcing community involvement*, The Policy Press.

Findings 320: 'Resourcing community involvement in neighbourhood regeneration'

The government's National Strategy for Neighbourhood Renewal places great importance on local communities playing a central role in securing a better quality of life for themselves. This study examined the way community involvement in such neighbourhoods is currently resourced. It highlights the strategic and financial gaps and puts forward specific proposals on how these might be filled.

Dyson, Alan and Robson, Elaine (1999) *School, family, community: Mapping school inclusion in the UK*, National Youth Agency.

Findings N19: 'Links between school, family and the community: a review of the evidence'

Mog Ball's (1998) report for the Joseph Rowntree Foundation – *Schooling inclusion* – described current practice in school–family–community links in the UK. New work from the University of Newcastle compliments the earlier report by reviewing the literature in this field in order to identify the effects and effectiveness of different types of link.

Edwards, Bill and Goodwin, Mark (2000) *Partnership working in rural regeneration: Governance and empowerment*, The Policy Press.

Findings 039: 'Partnership working in rural regeneration'

Partnership working is an increasingly important vehicle for the implementation of rural development policy. However, little is known about how partnerships work in practice. This project, from a team at the University of Wales, studied partnerships active in rural regeneration to explore how the effectiveness of partnership working might be improved.

Fitzpatrick, Suzanne; Hastings, Annette and Kintrea, Keith (1998) *Including young people in urban regeneration: A lot to learn?*, The Policy Press.

Findings 918: 'Including young people in urban regeneration'

As the difficulties faced by young people living within disadvantaged communities have become increasingly apparent, youth issues have gained prominence within area-based regeneration initiatives. This study, by a team from the University of Glasgow, investigated the extent to which urban regeneration projects have met the needs of young people aged 16-24 years old, and how young people have become involved as active participants in these initiatives. A training pack for youth workers and young people, based on the lessons from this project, is in preparation.

Forrest, Ray and Kearns, Ade (1999) *Joined-up places? Social cohesion and neighbourhood regeneration*, York Publishing Services.

Findings 4109: 'Social cohesion and urban inclusion for disadvantaged neighbourhoods'

Four research projects in Teesside, London, Liverpool and Nottingham studied the physical and social qualities of disadvantaged neighbourhoods and the interaction between them. They considered the factors affecting social cohesion within neighbourhoods and how this might strengthen. They also looked at what residents themselves felt about their neighbourhoods and the impact of the area regeneration initiatives. This report provides an overview of the four projects. The reports of the individual projects (authored by Wood and Vamplew – Teesside, Cattell and Evans – London, Andersen and Munck – Liverpool and Silburn et al – Nottingham) are also included in this list.

Green, Ann and Owen, David (1998) *Where are the jobless? Changing unemployment and non-employment in cities and regions*, The Policy Press.

Findings 408: 'Geographical variations in unemployment and non-employment'

Unemployment is only part of *non-employment, with inactivity* being the other part. This research, by a team based at the University of Warwick, indicates a more pronounced a more regional pattern on non-employment than of unemployment, which policies need to take into account.

Gregory, Sarah (1998) *Transforming local services: partnership in action*, York Publishing Services.

Findings HR248: 'The effectiveness of local service partnerships on disadvantaged estates'

Residents on the poorest estates suffer disproportionaly high levels of disadvantage. Their needs and problems are complex and often fall outside the scope of responsibility of any one service. This study looked at the concept of 'local service partnerships' which aim to collect all local service delivery agencies and to bring these agencies and the communities together. The project, which contributed to Government's current interest in Neighbourhood Management, looked in detail at case studies in Coventry and Burnley.

Hall, Stephen and Mawson, John (1999) *Challenge funding, contracts and area regeneration: A decade of innovation, policy management and co-ordination*, The Policy Press.

Findings 359: 'Lessons for area regeneration from policy development in the 1990s'

The limited success of area regeneration policies is, in part, due to the fragmented nature of governance nationally and locally. This study charts the illusion of area regeneration policy in the 1990s. A key focus of this activity has been to improve coordination for local initiatives.

Hawtin, Murray et al (1999) *Housing integration and resident participation: Evaluation of a project to help integrate black and ethnic minority tenants*, York Publishing Services.

This study is an evaluation of a tenant participation project led by Unity Housing Association which sought to integrate black and minority ethnic tenants (from inner city areas in Leeds) into two existing peripheral council estates where new developments were being undertaken jointly by Unity and two other housing associations.

Henderson, Paul and Mayo, Marjorie (1998) *Training and education in urban regeneration: A framework for participants*, The Policy Press.

Training and education are key to the success of area-based regeneration. Capacity building has already been recognised as vital if communities are to play an effective role. But it is not only communities that are in need of training and education. This report makes the case for developing a strategic approach to training and education for all stakeholders engaged in area regeneration, including: policy makers, professionals and local residents.

Low, John (1998)

Foundations HF588: 'Regenerating neighbourhoods: creating integrated and sustainable improvements'

This Foundations summarises lessons from JRF research since 1992 into what works in the regeneration of deprived neighbourhoods. The research findings show that each area is different with its own unique problems and opportunities. Local initiatives must be allowed the room to *grow* and find their own ways of responding to local needs and priorities. Nevertheless, JRF research also highlights clear similarities in the key issues and processes that all regeneration initiatives must address. It also identifies if they are to succeed, what local, regional and central government must do to support neighbourhood efforts.

Low, John (1999)

Summary 169: 'Developing effective community involvement strategies'

This summary document was produced on the basis of all the work that the Joseph Rowntree Foundation had done since 1992 on the role of local residents and community organisations in urban regeneration. It was prepared at the request of the Department of the Environment, Transport and the Regions, and produced to coincide with Round 6 of the Single Regeneration Budget. Based on previous JRF research, the document concluded that, prior to developing SRB bids, it is essential for partnership to develop Community Involvement Strategies to outline methods for involving residents and local organisations before, during and after SRB programmes. The document also identifies all key stages in the work of preparing, establishing and monitoring Community Involvement Strategies.

Macfarlane, Richard (1997) *Unshackling the poor: A complementary approach to local economic development,* York Publishing Services.

As the industrial structure of the UK has changed, many people will face a future of insecure employment, often in temporary and low-paid jobs, with frequent spells of unemployment. This report considers creative ways of relieving social and economic exclusion. The report examines new approaches to local economic development beyond current preoccupations with job creation, business development and training. It suggests that these approaches can be complementary to other activities aimed at securing economic and social regeneration. In particular, the report focuses on the benefit system, the informal economy, voluntary action and self-help activities.

Macfarlane, Richard (2000) *Local jobs from local development: The use of Planning Agreements to target training and employment outcomes,* York Publishing Services.

Findings 350: Using planning agreements to reduce social exclusion

This study examines the potential for using local authority planning and development control powers to target the training and employment opportunities generated by new developments at disadvantaged communities. Based on an analysis of the current legal position, a survey of current local authority activity and four case studies, the work concludes that there is scope for wider use of the relevant powers and that this is a valid way of achieving 'sustainable development' and ensuring that new developments make a contribution to reducing social exclusion.

Macfarlane, Richard (2000) *Using local labour in construction: A good practice resource book,* The Policy Press.

Findings N80: 'Local labour in construction: tackling social exclusion and skill shortages'

This report looks at targeting local labour into construction and, thus, building local capacity. The author argues that effective schemes are difficult to establish in a fast-moving and fragmented industry. The report brings together the experience of 25 local initiatives to provide good practice guidelines on what to do, how to do it and outlines what it is possible for initiatives to achieve.

Maclennan, Duncan (2000) *Changing places, engaging people,* York Publishing Services.

The JRF Area Regeneration Programme encompasses more than 50 diverse research and development studies of the problems in, and possible solutions for, rejuvenating deprived areas. In this report Duncan Maclennan relates the key findings from the programme to the Social Exclusion Unit's National Strategy for Neighbourhood Renewal. The author pays special attention to the role of housing systems in neighbourhood change; the need for a more sophisticated understanding of how labour markets work and how regeneration programmes interact with these.

May, Nicky (1997) *Challenging assumptions: Gender issues in urban regeneration,* York Publishing Services.

This report explores how women and men experience poverty and exclusion differently, and some reasons behind these differences. It looks at patterns of social disadvantage in urban areas, how community members perceive women's and men's roles, and whether policy makers take account of changing roles in the workplace and at home. The study finds that women are generally more vulnerable than men in the same circumstances. It finds evidence that regeneration practitioners often overlook women's concerns due to unquestioned assumptions about the social and economic roles of women and men, and that this reduces the effectiveness of urban regeneration initiatives.

Mayo, Ed; Fisher, Thomas; Conaty, Pat; Doling, John and Millineux, Andy (1998) *Small is bankable: Community reinvestment in the UK*, Joseph Rowntree Foundation.

Findings N38: 'Community reinvestment in the UK'

There is a stark and growing finance gap in disadvantaged neighbourhoods as public funding declines but private investment has not taken its place. Community finance initiatives have emerged to tackle this gap. They start from a single idea: that people in groups excludedfrom or invisible to mainstream finance can still be bankable. The study was carried out by a team from the New Economics Foundation.

McGlone, Pauline; Dobson, Barbara; Dowler, Elizabeth and Nelson, Michael (1999) *Food projects and how they work*, York Publishing Services.

Findings 329: 'Food projects and how they work'

The government programme to reduce health and social inequalities is encouraging communities to develop sustainable initiatives to address local problems. One example of this is local food projects, but, to date, there has been little systematic research on how these work. This study draws on the experience of 25 food projects to give a better understanding of how these projects work, what they can realistically be expected to achieve and, most importantly, how they can help.

McGregor, Alan; Glass, Andrea; Richmond, Kenneth; Ferguson, Zoe and Higgins, Kevin (1999) *Employer involvement in area regeneration*, The Policy Press.

Findings 839: 'Getting employers involved in area regeneration'

Securing sustainable area economic regeneration has been difficult. It is increasingly recognised that the employing community has a key role to play in the process. This study, by a team at the University of Glasgow, researched the effectiveness of a range of area regeneration projects where employers made a significant input and explored how this effectiveness might be improved.

Newcombe, Richard (1998) *Not too big, not too small: Strategies for medium-sized housing associations*, Centre for Housing Policy, York.

Findings 958: 'Future strategies for medium-sized housing associations'

The future for medium-sized housing associations (between 250-2500 homes) is very uncertain. A particular issue is their willingness and scope for diversification through 'Housing Plus' activities into a broader community role. This study has examined the options open to such associations, structural frameworks within which they are working and their perceptions of the future.

Niner, Pat (1999)

Foundations 739: 'Insights into low demand for housing'

In this Foundations, Pat Niner draws on a number of recent research projects supported by the Joseph Rowntree Foundation which give insight into the phenomenon of 'low demand' for housing stock.

Oc, Tanner; Tiesdell, Steven and Moynihan, David (1997) *Urban regeneration and ethnic minority groups: Training and business support in City Challenge areas*, The Policy Press.

Findings H227: 'Urban regeneration and ethnic minority groups: training and business support in City Challenge areas'

This study looked at training provision and business support services in six City Challenge areas with substantial minority ethnic populations and where efforts were made to address the needs and problems faced by minority ethnic groups.

Parkinson, Michael (1998) *Combating social exclusion: Lessons from area-based programmes in Europe*, The Policy Press.

Findings 838: 'Combating social exclusion: lessons from area-based programmes in Europe'

This study, by a team at Liverpool John Moores University, assesses the development of national strategies for area-based responses to social exclusion in four major cities in France, Denmark, the Netherlands and Ireland. On the basis of the experiences in these four countries, the policy implications for Britain are discussed.

Platt, Lucinda and Noble, Michael (1999) *Race, place and poverty: Ethnic groups and low income distribution*, York Publishing Services.

Findings 249: 'Ethnic groups and low income distribution'

This study, by a team from the University of Oxford, is based in Birmingham. Using recent data, the study shows great diversity in the experience of those on low income, according to their ethnic group. The study defined low income as being in receipt of the mean-tested Housing Benefit and/or Council Tax Benefit and concentrated on four groups: white UK, Bangladeshi, black Caribbean and Pakistani.

Plummer, John and Zipfel, Tricia (1998) *Regeneration and employment: A new agenda for TECS, communities and partnerships*, The Policy Press.

Findings 328: 'The role of TECs and LECs in regeneration'

Training and Enterprise Councils (TECs or LECs in Scotland) are expected to be important players in urban regeneration, providing expertise and economic development private sector involvement within a partnership framework. The study looks at the role of TECs and LECs in six areas and explores the factors that support and inhibit the development of partnership working.

Power, Anne and Mumford, Katharine (1999) *The slow death of great cities? Urban abandonment or urban renaissance*, York Publishing Services.

Findings 519: 'The problem of low housing demand in inner city areas

In some inner city areas there is virtually no demand foe housing. Anne Power and Katharine Mumford, in a detailed study of such neighbourhoods, found that the reasons were more to do with severe poverty and joblessness within the neighbourhoods than the quality of the housing. The study found that intensive inputs on many fronts are helping to stabilise conditions in these communities.

Purdue, Derrick; Razzaque, Konica; Hambleton, Robin and Stewart, Murray, with Huxham, Chris and Vangan, Siv (2000) *Community leadership in area regeneration*, The Policy Press.

Findings 720: 'Strengthening community leaders in area regeneration'

Successful regeneration projects depend on effective community involvement. This study examines the role and impact of community leaders involved in area regeneration partnerships. The researchers looked at the role of community leaders in SRB schemes in nine case studies in the UK. The analysis suggests a bold change is needed if the rhetoric about community involvement is to be matched by good practice on the ground.

Richardson, Keith and Corbishley, Peter (1999) *Frequent moving: Looking for love?*, York Publishing Services.

Findings 439: 'The characteristics of frequent movers'

Some families move as often as three times a year. Both residents and housing workers see this as contributing to the decline of an area. In a small-scale exploratory study of tenants in the West End of Newcastle, the researchers found evidence to suggest that this pattern has its origins in childhood or adolescent experiences, and is not necessarily the result of either economic factors or illegal activity.

Robinson, David; Dunn, Kathryn and Ballintyne, Scott (1998) *Social Enterprise Zones: Building innovation into regeneration*, York Publishing Services.

Summary 0128: 'Social Enterprise Zones'

Improvements in the national economy barely impact on areas suffering from the worst multiple deprivation. A network of Social Enterprise Zones could provide a framework for delivering the New Deal for Communities and has the potential to connect Employment, Health and Education zones. This study examines in depth, the concept of the Social Enterprise Zone as developed by the Community Links agency in East London. The report was based on a review of relevant research and on consultation with academics, policy makers and practitioners.

Robson, Brian; Peck, Jamie and Holden, Adam (2000) *Regional agencies and area-based regeneration*, The Policy Press.

Findings 550: 'Regional Development Agencies and local regeneration'

This study of the eight Regional Development Agencies in England aim to assess the progress being made in developing regional agendas and to see what impact the new structures of regional government are having on local regeneration practice.

Russell, Hilary (1998) *A place for the community? Tyne and Wear Development Corporation's approach to regeneration*, The Policy Press.

Findings 548: 'Community development: the Tyne and Wear Development Corporation's approach'

Property-led regeneration programmes are often assumed to neglect the interests of adjacent deprived communities. A study by Liverpool John Moores University examined the claim by the Tyne and Wear Development Corporation that it implemented a community development strategy which enabled local communities to participate in and benefit from its regeneration programmes.

Sanderson, Ian, with Walton, Fiona and Campbell, Mike (1999) *Back to work: Local action on unemployment*, Work and Opportunities Programme, York Publishing Services.

Findings 629: 'Local action on unemployment'

Policies to address long-term unemployment, at European, national and, increasingly, regional levels are giving greater weight to local action tailored to conditions in specific labour markets. This study presents the results of detailed case study research to investigate what forms of local action are effective in getting people into work and how local schemes should be organised to address the needs of individuals, groups and localities.

Silburn, Richard; Lucas, Dan; Page, Robert and Hanna, Lynn (1999) *Neighbourhood images in Nottingham: Social cohesion and neighbourhood change*, York Publishing Services.

Findings 489: 'Neighbourhood images in Nottingham'

The adjacent Nottingham inner-city neighbourhoods of Hyson Green and Forest Fields are areas of long-standing multiple disadvantage and have a negative image in the city. However, research reveals that local residents take considerable pride in that area. They point to many positive features which could contribute to policies of area regeneration. This project was carried out in parallel with three other similar projects in Teesside, London and Liverpool; an overview report of all four projects was written out by Ray Forrest and Ade Kearns.

Smith, Paula and Patterson, Bob (1999) *Making it all add up: Housing associations and community investment*, York Publishing Services.

Findings 959: 'Housing association investment in people'

Activities which aim to make communities more sustainable have been referred to as 'Housing Plus', 'added value' and 'community investment'. This research, carried out for the umbrella group People for Action, examined the community investment activities of a wide range of housing associations.

Speak, Suzanne and Graham, Steve (2000) *Service not included: Social implications of private sector restructuring in marginalised neighbourhoods*, The Policy Press.

Findings 230: 'Private sector service withdrawal in disadvantaged neighbourhoods'

Privatisation and restructuring have left less affluent neighbourhoods and social groups with only limited access to services which could be considered essential for full participation in contemporary society. This study, by the University of Newcastle, looks at access to energy, telephones, banking and food retailing to marginalised neighbourhoods.

Taylor, Marilyn (2000) *Top down meets bottom up: Neighbourhood Management*, Joseph Rowntree Foundation.

Summary 310: 'Tackling social exclusion at local level: Neighbourhood Management'

Neighbourhood Management is one of the 'big ideas' in the government's campaign to tackle social exclusion and forms a key part of its National Strategy for Neighbourhood Renewal. But how will it work? And will it make a difference? This reports asks what we have learnt from experience so far. It spells out the key themes that Neighbourhood Management needs to address and sums up the most promising ideas that are coming out of practice and research.

Turok, Ivan and Edge, Nicola (1999) *The jobs gap in Britain's cities: Employment loss and labour market consequences*, The Policy Press.

Findings 569: 'The jobs gap in Britain's cities'

There has been no systematic analysis of employment trends in Britain's cities for a decade. Many government policies do not recognise the significance of widening geographical disparities in labour market conditions. This study, by a team at the University of Glasgow, examined urban economic change over the last two decades and the impact on local people.

Ward, Michael (1997) *Here to stay: A public policy framework for community-based regeneration*, Development Trusts Association.

Summary (no number): 'A public policy framework for community-based regeneration'

Neighbourhood-based renewal agencies, which grew from local campaign organisations, have won wide acceptance as a vehicle for tackling the effects of multiple deprivation and social exclusion in some of our most marginalised communities. These effects include unemployment, poverty, environmental blight and crime. This study, carried out for the Development Trust Association, examined the current role of 150 community-based regeneration organisations in these communities.

Williams, Colin C. and Windebank, Jan (1999) *A helping hand: Harnessing self-help to combat social exclusion*, York Publishing Services.

Findings 859: 'Harnessing self-help to combat social exclusion'

This study considers whether helping people to help themselves and others can be developed as an additional tool for tackling social exclusion to complement job creation. The researchers surveyed 400 households in deprived neighbourhoods of Southampton and Sheffield to examine the current extent of their self-help activity, the barriers to people doing more for themselves and others, and how these might be overcome.

Wolman, Harold and Page, Edward C. (2000) *Learning from the experience of others: Policy transfer among local regeneration partnerships*, York Publishing Service.

Findings 530: 'Policy transfer between local regeneration partnerships'

A variety of government, non-profit and private sector organisations have sought to encourage the flow of ideas and services between regeneration initiatives across the country. This new survey of regeneration partnerships (all based within local authorities) examined if and how local policy makers use this information. It provides useful lessons about how local officials learn (or don't learn) from previous experience in other cities.

Wood, Martin and Vamplew, Clive (1999) *Neighbourhood images in Teesside: Regeneration or decline?*, York Publishing Services.

Findings 469: 'Neighbourhood images in Teesside'

A qualitative assessment of the views of people living in two estates in Teesside reveals that stigma and social exclusion have remained despite expensive regeneration initiatives. Both of the areas studied had a long history of disadvantage and had remained unpopular. The researchers explored residents' perceptions of life on the estates, their views of regeneration and their future hopes and expectations. This project ran in parallel to three other similar projects in London, Liverpool and Nottingham; an overview report of all four projects was written by Ray Forrest and Ade Kearns.

Area Regeneration Programme projects still in progress

Note: Details of prospective publishers in this section are accurate at time of going to press but are subject to possible change.

Bevan, Mark and Gilroy, Rose *Urban Parish Councils*, York Publishing Services.

This study will look at the formation of an urban parish council in one ward of Newcastle. The researchers will review the literature on the subject of urban parish councils and examine: the case for establishing an Urban Parish Council in Newcastle; the difficulties encountered in attempting to realise this plan; and possibly, the early achievements of this urban parish council.

McGillivray, Alex (and others) *Low flying heroes*, New Economics Foundation.

This study focuses on 'micro-social enterprise'- namely very small, often informal, voluntary organisations. The researchers estimate that there may be anywhere between 600,000-900,000 of them in the U.K. These 'low flying heroes' which thrive in adversity, are informal groups, usually motivated by social and environment benefits, who make a real contribution to social inclusion, neighbourhood renewal and sustainable communities.

McGregor, Alan *Achieving greater integration of area regeneration and social inclusion strategies*, The Policy Press.

This study examines the case for improved collaboration between government programmes which focus on *individuals* (for example, New Deal for Work) and those which focus on *communities* (for example, SRB programmes). The study will look at both the advantages and disadvantages of achieving greater coordination between these two different types of programme.

Parkinson, Michael and Russell, Hilary *An evaluation of the New Commitment to Regeneration*

This study, jointly funded by JRF, DETR and the Local Government Association, is an evaluation of LGA's New Commitment to Regeneration. The focus is on the 22 'pathfinder' local authorities who are currently involved in this initiative. The project, due to complete in 2001, will examine progress in the Pathfinders in achieving new forms of 'joined-up' working which link closely to Government policies such as Modernising Local Government and the National Strategy for Neighbourhood Renewal.

Robinson, David and Smerdon, Matthew *Next steps for social enterprise zones*

This project is a follow-on from the project (by the same researchers) referenced in the main list above. While the previous project was in the nature of a 'thinkpiece', this project tracks the development of a Social Enterprise Zone 'for real' in an East London borough. The project will look at the needs of a very deprived area of East London, characterised by high levels of unemployment and a heavy reliance on the public purse. The project will document efforts to define more creative and effective ways of using this heavy public spend in walls that help local residents to find routes out of unemployment and deprivation,

Saunders, Roger (and others) *Resident Services Organisations*

An earlier project for the JRF by Roger Saunders of PEP Limited looked at the French concept of the 'Regie de Quartier'. This is a form of local business, supported by social landlords in France, which allows them to employ tenants to carry out essential functions on housing estates, such as repairs and landscaping works. This project is an attempt to pilot the concept (renamed Resident Services Organisations) on this side of the Channel. Roger Saunders is helping two RSOs , one in London and one in Brighton. The report will give an account of how the project has fared on two social housing estates.

Thake, Steven *Building communities, changing lives: The contribution of large, independent neighbourhood regeneration organisations*

This report summarises the findings of a study of large, independent neighbourhood-based regeneration organisations. The study builds on previous work commissioned by JRF and seeks to cover four main areas: to examine the contribution that these large neighbourhood organisations can make to tackling social exclusion; to assess whether particular models of neighbourhood organisations can be matched to particular types of disadvantaged neighbourhood; to provide guidelines to practitioners and policy makers about selecting the most appropriate model of community regeneration organisation; and to recommend possible changes in: funding arrangements, regulatory frameworks and government policies.